I0168273

Copyright © 2013 by Simon Webber

All rights reserved.

No part of this book may be reproduced in any form or by any
electronic or mechanical means including information storage and
retrieval systems, without permission in writing from the author.
The only exception is by a reviewer, who may quote short excerpts
in a review.

Simon Webber

Printed in the United Kingdom

First printing 19 June 2014

ISBN 978-0-9929238-0-8

This isn't a book in the accepted sense. It's a collection of fictitious, humorous letters that might have been written by, (or in some cases to,) the appropriate health and safety directorate in bygone days.

There are 60 letters in all, concerning a variety of actual or imaginary events. Where actual, each has been researched as far as possible to achieve a degree of authenticity.

Elah Valley Health and Safety Directorate

Council Offices, 23 -27 High Street, Valley Trading Estate, Socoh, Judah

Mr Jesse (the Bethlehemite)
c/o The Israelite Army Headquarters
Elah Valley, Judah   2nd February 980 B.C.

Dear Mr Jesse

We have been made aware by the Philistines that your son, David, is due to take part in a one-to-one contest with Mr Goliath of Gath in the Elah Valley next Wednesday at 3 p.m. We are contacting you as your son is a minor, and therefore not legally responsible for his actions. We understand that your son's only weapon will be a sling and some small stones, which he uses to scare wolves away from his flock.

Mr Goliath has pointed out that while he considers your son to be, in his own words, " a puny, circumcised little twerp he can beat with one arm tied behind my back", he believes David's use of small but possibly sharp stones to be a dangerous practice, and to contravene Health and Safety regulations.

This is the case. However, we recognise that your son is of small stature in relation to Mr Goliath, and while we need to ensure adherence to the regulations, the Directorate does not wish to ban David's weapon altogether. So we write to notify you that David would not be contravening the aforesaid regulations if he replaces his stones with pieces of camel dung for the contest. This is plentiful in the area.

While you might initially feel that camel dung is of too soft a consistency to have any effect on impact, our tests have shown that dung from female camels in heat, properly moulded, shaped, and kept in the sun for 3-4 days, has virtually the consistency of stone.

We must remain impartial in this matter, but you might wish to know that not only do these projectiles have excellent penetrating power, but also, if they don't disable Mr Goliath, will instantly make him irresistible to all the male camels in the area. So we don't think he'll have time to win the contest!

Yours faithfully,

Ibrahim Abdullah

Health and Safety Directorate

Mr Archimedes
Discovery House
27-29 The Grand Parade
West Syracuse   2nd September 265 B.C.

Dear Mr Archimedes

I write firstly to congratulate you on your recent discovery of water displacement as an accurate indicator of volume, and how, using this discovery, you were able to determine the purity of the gold in President Hiero's crown.

As an amateur scientist myself (in my spare time of course), I was fascinated to hear both of your discovery and that it resulted from your immersing yourself in your bath and accurately measuring the increase in water depth.

Your discovery has of course received widespread publicity, and this had necessitated our writing to you on some health and safety issues.

Firstly, we have received reports that, clearly without fully understanding the concept, many members of the public have used the bath water displacement procedure to try and check the purity of their gold possessions. Here is a typical example. A Mr Pythagoras of North Syracuse immersed his wife Aphrodite naked in their bath and marked the water level. He then got her to put on all her gold jewellery and immersed her a second time. Unfortunately, the weight of the gold immediately sent her to the bottom of the bath. As Mr Pythagoras was concentrating on comparing the water levels it was only swift action by a servant in pulling the bath plug that saved her life.

As our second case illustrates, publishing discoveries like yours often motivates the lunatic fringe. A Mr Hippocrates of 23 Argonaut Road assumed that your discovery method could be used to check the difference between the water displacement of his penis at rest, and when it was fully erect. He decided to do this in front of the lady he was trying to impress. Unfortunately, he failed to take into account that the bathwater he was using was cold, and the net difference between the water levels was actually negative.

Consequently he has not only lost his girlfriend but is receiving counselling by the Syracuse Sex Clinic.

Encouraging the public to submerge themselves in their baths is contrary to our health and safety guidelines. In this instance we will simply issue you a warning not to publicise any other bath immersion activities.

The second health and safety matter concerns the fact that, immediately following your discovery, you apparently rushed into the street and ran the length of Appian Avenue totally naked.

It appears that some members of the public were more impressed with this than with your actual discovery. Syracuse police have notified us of a big increase in "streaking" in the area. As you can imagine, this has caused great shock and distress to female residents, and has lead to a large number of complaints. I quote from a representative letter from a Mrs Ambrosia, a senior member of the Vestal Virgins (Syracuse branch), who wrote: *" I was out shopping last Thursday, and I saw four naked male streakers in the space of a morning. It was absolutely disgusting. And I had to run all the way up Poseidon Street in order not to miss the last one"*.

Here again, as you are a respected citizen and scientist, we would be happy to conclude this matter with a warning not to repeat your above action.

Yours faithfully

Hippocrates the younger

Junior Health and Safety Officer

South Essex Health & Safety Directorate

Safety House, 57-60 High Street, Colchester, Essex

The Hon. William Harbottel-Grimston, Kt.
Justice of the Peace
The Court House
Chelmsford Village   14th November 1696

Your Lordship,

May I first say how sorry we were to hear about your being struck down with severe constipation. We all here wish you a speedy recovery.

We are writing to you is about one of your current cases. This involves 57 year old Miss Elizabeth Horner, sentenced by Your Lordship at the quarter sessions yesterday to the 'Ducking Stool', to prove whether or not she is a witch. As you know, this will involve strapping Miss Horner to a wooden chair suspended from a beam and then 'ducking' her beneath the surface of the River Chel several times.

So that there is no risk of Miss Horner drowning, we understand that Your Lordship has graciously agreed that she may be given a hollow stick through which to breathe while under the water. We are satisfied this meets her health and safety welfare in this matter.

However, Miss Horner vehemently states that there is no evidence that she is a witch, and that your sentence should be annulled. We think Your Lordship should know that Miss Horner has now also admitted that following your sentencing, she cast a spell on you preventing you evacuating your bowels. Hence perhaps your condition.

Miss Horner is not prepared to undo the spell unless you annul her sentence, and has made a somewhat bold suggestion as to what Your Lordship might do with the hollow stick!! (Funnily enough, what she proposes might actually be a means of alleviating your discomfort.)

May we have Your Lordship's comments on Miss Horner's demand.

Yours faithfully

William Toppley

Health and Safety Director

WEST KASSEL HEALTH & SAFETY DIRECTORATE
OUNCIL OFFICES, 286-300 PUMPERNICKEL STRASSE, KASSEL, GERMANY

Squadron Leader G. Winton-Smith
Senior Escape Officer (British)
Oflag 1X, Spangenberg Castle, Kassel   20th October 1941

Dear Squadron Leader,

We understand that you are planning another escape attempt from Oflag 1X. While, under the Geneva Convention, you have the right to try to escape, we must point out that any such attempts must not contravene the Kassel Health & Safety regulations. In this connection may we draw your attention to the following:-

Firstly, in the event that you again choose to site the entrance for your tunnel beneath one of the barrack room lavatories, be aware that your tunnellers returning to the barracks via the lavatory concerned must give a clear signal no less than one minute before emerging.

Secondly, you must affix warning notices on the relevant seat, drawing attention to the toilet's additional use. The specific wording must be concise, as follows:

"ATTENTION - If you intend to use this lavatory, be aware that your motions could be interrupted. If, while seated, you hear two taps coming from beneath the lavatory, it indicates that a tunneller will shortly appear beneath your buttocks. The timing of your motions therefore needs to be strictly controlled, and you should be ready to evacuate your position immediately".

These notices must not only be in English but also German, in case one of the camp guards needs to relieve himself on the lavatory concerned. (As you will be aware, this actually happened to Feldwebel Kopfsheitzer during your previous attempt, and the absence of any warning notices caused the Feldwebel shock and distress for which he is still receiving counselling). Also in this connection, perhaps you would pass on our best wishes for a speedy recovery to Pilot Officer Smith, who, we understand, was the tunneller involved.

Please immediately acknowledge these instructions and your agreement.

Yours faithfully

Adolph Turpitzufer

Health & Safety Executive

Greater London Health and Safety Executive

FLOOR 29, CENTRE POINT, NEW OXFORD STREET, LONDON WC1

Mr Reginald Thomas
Complaints Manager
Lifelike Inflatable Dolls (London) Ltd
378-380 Great West Road
London WT9 6TB

28th October 1997

Dear Mr Thomas

We are writing to you following health and safety complaints we have received from a number of your mail-order customers. Here are two representative examples :-.

Case 1. This concerns Mr Hugo Froggat, of 23 Station Road, Croydon, and his recent purchase of your "Big Wendy" blow-up doll complete with inflation pump, (product model E24). Mr Froggat has pointed out that he chose "Big Bertha" because the model features separate upper and lower inflation valves, allowing him to tailor the doll's shape to his personal requirements. (Since his preference is for ladies with large buttocks, this product feature would allow him to add extra air pressure to this part of the doll).

While erecting "Big Bertha" Mr Froggat was sitting with the doll on his lap carrying out this final buttocks inflation. This is when the incident occurred. There was a sudden, violent, downward 'punch' of warm air to Mr Froggat's groin (which, incidentally he did not consider an unpleasant sensation at the time). This was unfortunately later found to have caused a hernia.

Mr Froggat insists that he did not excessively inflate "Big Bertha", and this is the case. After inspecting the doll, our technical division discovered a fault in one of its thigh seams.

From a health and safety viewpoint we feel there's a lack of adequate guidance on this point for purchasers seeking to erect the doll. Therefore, if you wish to continue to market your "Big Bertha" model, you must include the following bold text within the instruction leaflet:- '**WARNING - Do not sit with 'Big Bertha' on your lap while attempting an erection'.**

Case 2. This concerns pensioner Mr Henry Smith who lives with his 85 year old wife at 34 Heath View, Putney W12. Both are poorly sighted.

Some months ago Mr Smith purchased your "Mature Mabel" (product model M32 with inflation pump). While his wife was out shopping, he followed your erection instructions and then sat the doll on the sofa. (On her return Mrs Smith, who had left her glasses in the chemist's, noticed the figure and assumed that her sister had come to stay).

Later that evening, concerned that "Mature Mabel" was becoming somewhat deflated, Mr Smith started to connect the pump. Mrs Smith had been dozing in her armchair, and it was only her screams that alerted him to the fact that he was inadvertently trying to attach the pump to his wife's navel.

In line with health and safety regulations, we require you to include the following notice in your instructions :-. "**Before attaching the inflation pump, first pinch the valve on the doll sharply between thumb and forefinger. If you are attempting to connect to the wrong fixture, this will immediately become evident**".

Yours faithfully

Cyril Crumble

Senior Health and Safety Inspector

DEUTSCHE HEALTH UND SAFETY DIRECTORATE

WESTERN FRONT SECTION, 34 RUE DU COCHON BLEU, MONS, FRANCE

Field Marshall Sir Douglas Haig CBE, DSO, DFC
Commander in Chief – Western Front
British Expeditionary Force
Nr Bapaume, France   25th April 1916

Dear Field Marshall,

Please accept the apologies of our Directorate for troubling you at a time when you are heavily involved with the forthcoming battle of the Somme, (oh yes, we know all about this!) But there is a serious health and safety matter that requires your urgent attention.

We are aware that, under battle conditions, lacking other means of communication your front line troops frequently adopt the practice of releasing carrier pigeons from your trenches to convey messages to your headquarters. We have received complaints from the German front line troops in the Bapaume region that, while flying over their lines, British pigeons frequently defecate.

Unlike mortars or artillery shells, there is no audible warning of these insidious projectiles. If our troops look up while your pigeons pass overhead, these projectiles can hit them in the face, causing eye damage and skin inflammation. This has become known by our German troops as 'Englische Himmel Scheisse'.

Furthermore, our Directorate's livestock officer, (whose personal hobby is pigeons), has pointed out that when your British Expeditionary Force arrived in France, the breed of pigeons your troops brought with them, 'Colomba Britannica', have small bowels.

However, those that your troops have subsequently caught and trained in France and Belgium are 'Colomba Europa', a breed with significantly larger bowel capacity.

Our German front line troops see this as an unfair form of warfare, and a dangerous practice, with which we concur. You are therefore required to take both of the following actions immediately prior to any further pigeon release :-

a) The supervising officer must personally ensure that each pigeon is squeezed gently but firmly, (using no less than 23 lbs per square inch), to evacuate any bowel content.

b) The supervising officer must then attach a small 'nappy', (a paper facemask is ideal), to the rear of the pigeon, hooked over the wings to keep it in place. This will retain any droppings during flight. We have successfully tested this method, which shows that while the pigeons are startled when the 'nappies' are initially fitted, they soon become used to them. It is also true that at the end of a long flight, the extra weight carried may sometimes result in a heavy landing. However, we feel this is a small price to pay to protect the well-being of our German troops.

Please confirm your agreement to adopt these health and safety instructions by return.

Yours faithfully,

Herman Pickelhelm

German Health and Safety Directorate

P.S. Your secret trials of chickens and turkeys for this same dastardly role are also known to us, and these trials must cease immediately.

The English Health and Safety Directorate
Seventh Floor, Southdown House, Piccadilly, London SW1, England

Madam Marie Tucek
23 Rue de la Paix
Quatrieme Arrondisement
Paris, France   1st September 1893

Dear Madame Tucek

We are writing about your recent invention of the 'breast supporter' (or 'brassiere' as it is being called). Quoting from your literature, this product will 'lift and project the breasts'. We have obtained samples of your product and have sought the advice of our leading English structural engineer, Mr Isambard Brunel, as to health and safety aspects.

We quote from Mr Brunel's advice, as follows:- *"Following the challenges I faced in designing the Clifton Suspension Bridge, I am keenly aware of structural loading limitations. Regarding Madame Tucek's invention, to take two objects that would normally hang close to the body, but lift them upwards and outwards till they are suspended at 80-90 degrees from the vertical, will, in my view, lead to an overloading of the human spine. Had I adopted a similar loading for the Clifton Bridge, the first span would have collapsed into the Avon."*

On the basis of these professional comments, we consider your invention to be a serious health and safety risk to the English public. If you wish to sell your products here, we can see only one way in which English women can be protected from these risks. To balance the spinal loading, you will need to sell two 'breast supporters' to each client.

These must be accompanied by instructions that the wearer of the front-facing supporter must, at the same time, also wear a rear-facing version, with the fabric pockets of the rear version filled with the equivalent weight of a harmless substance such as sugar or flour to balance the loading. We hope the following weight guide will be helpful:-

Cup size (up to)	Sugar (per cup) (Tablespoons)	Flour (per cup) (Tablespoon)
32 B	2	3
36 B	3.5	5
38 D	6	8

Please confirm that you will adopt the above instructions.

Yours faithfully,

Victoria Fortescue (Mrs)
Health and Safety Executive

Mount Sinai Health & Safety Directorate

Council Offices, The Parade, Mount Sinai, Canaan

Mr T. Moses
Chief Executive
Israelite Tribe
The Encampment, Mount Sinai   4th June 1251 B.C.

Dear Mr Moses

We are aware that you have only recently settled here with your Israelite slaves after a somewhat challenging crossing of the Red Sea escaping from the Egyptians. Consequently, you may not yet be fully conversant with our local Health & Safety regulations.

We are writing to point out that when you ascend Mount Sinai to meet someone called 'God', (as we understand you are planning to do next week), if you personally carry back some 'commandments' inscribed on ten tablets of stone, you will be in breach of Health & Safety regulations. For your information, this would contravene Section 12, Part 2, ('Hernia, Groin and Back Pain Injury Risks').

To avoid prosecution, we suggest that you make arrangements for the aforementioned 'commandments' to be reproduced on a lighter material, such as papyrus or clay, or perhaps have them tattooed on the heads of ten of your slaves, so that they'll be 'mobile' commandments. Alternatively, if you insist on stone, you must use a smaller typestyle so that these 'commandments' can be inscribed on not more than two tablets. We recommend the font 'Papyrus Narrow'.

One other thought - can your colleague, 'God', not pass on these commandments to you verbally, perhaps set to a popular tune such as 'Ten Green Bottles' or something similar, to aid memorability?

We await your urgent response to this directive.

Yours faithfully

Shimon Belshazzar

Health & Safety Executive

Norfolk Health and Safety Directorate
Second floor, Tudor House, Unthank Road, Norwich

Mr John Boddy, (Senior Gamekeeper)
The Estate of the Lord Chumbley-Choate Bart.
West Norfolk   3rd April, 1535

Dear Mr Boddy,

Thank you for your recent letter regarding the new male fashion accessory, the 'Codpiece', that is becoming very popular. (Indeed, His Gracious Majesty Henry himself has taken to appearing in public in one).

We are aware that Codpieces are not worn beneath any other garments, and that, while this makes urination easy by just unbuttoning the flaps, Codpieces are also popularly being used for carrying other possessions.

In view of your profession, it's therefore understandable that you have taken to keeping your small ferret, 'Wilfred', in your Codpiece while you are out carrying out your duties. As you pointed out, this little creature not only helps protect your genitalia against thorns and grazes but also insulates these sensitive parts in cold weather.

It is therefore all the more unfortunate that, according to your letter, while you were out trapping on the Estate last week, 'Wilfred', normally of a docile disposition, had unexpectedly scented a female ferret in season, and had gone berserk within the close confines of your Codpiece. It is hard to imagine a more unpleasant experience, and we can understand how you came to drop your loaded musket which discharged, severing part of your right ear.

While some might see padding your Codpiece with a live ferret to be a little irresponsible, as a rural Health and Safety Directorate this is not our view.

Having fully considered the situation, we agree with your complaint and will immediately be contacting all Codpiece makers in Norwich. On health and safety grounds our Directorate will instruct them to take the following action:-

a) Firstly, to stop making the present design of Codpiece with immediate effect. In future these items must be made with not one but two 'compartments'.

b) Secondly, to avoid confusion, one compartment must be embroidered 'Private Parts' (with internal access as well as external), and the second embroidered 'Other Possessions'. This second compartment must be of a robust, heavy-duty fabric.

Thank you for bringing this matter to our attention. We hope your groin and your hearing will both eventually recover, and His Majesty has graciously asked us to pass on his best wishes.

Yours sincerely,

William Overbury

Norfolk Health and Safety Executive

THE ROYAL COURT OF PHARAOH RAMESSES

SORCERERS AND MAGICIANS DEPARTMENT, THE ROYAL PALACE, THE MALL OF THE SPHINXES, THEBES

Mr Ali Hassan - Director
Egyptian Health and Safety Directorate
West Nile Avenue
Thebes   4th September 1257 B.C.

Dear Ali

Confidentially, as you and I are professional men, you will appreciate how frustrating it can be when we get amateur weirdoes like a yokel called 'Moses' who turning up at the Royal Court yesterday.

He did tricks in front of His Majesty like turning shepherds crooks into snakes, water into blood, and making his arm appear leprous. (His Majesty was quite impressed, but being in the business, I know that these are some of the first tricks you learn at the Central Sorcerers' School at Amarna).

I also understand that, last week, up on Mount Horeb he made a bush burn without destroying it! I'm not sure how he did that. But apparently he's got a chum called 'Gog or 'God' who's a wizard behind the scenes.

Ali, it's not so much that this 'Moses' is trying to upstage me at Court in front of His Majesty but, from a health and safety viewpoint, can you imaging what would happen if people went round setting fire to bushes and turning crooks into snakes. And you never know where this can lead.

Moses actually told His Majesty that if he wasn't allowed to take his people out of Egypt he'd do something really dramatic like 'parting the waters', but he wouldn't explain what he meant. (His Majesty was worried that this might refer to his planned surgery in Thebes Hospital next month to deal with his 'waterworks' problem).

I hope you'll agree that this 'Moses' should not be allowed to carry on this dangerous behaviour, and ban his activities without delay.

Mustapha

Mustapha Horemheb, Chief Magician

Mrs F. Godmother
c/o The Princess Lucinda ('previously 'Cinderella')
The Royal Palace, Fairyland   20th April in the year 1495

Dear Mrs Godmother

Your name is not on the local voting register, so we are sending this communication care of the Princess, who we understand is your relative. We are writing concerning a serious violation of Health and Safety regulations on your part. This results from a letter we've received from a Mr Gregory William Mouse.

As Mr Mouse states: *"On the 10th of this month, (the night of the Prince's Ball), I was going about my normal business with some other mice when there was a sudden flash and a bang. I found myself dressed in a coachmen's livery and sitting precariously on the box of a coach trying to control six black horses. It gave me a real turn, I can tell you."*

As Mr Mouse pointed out, he has never received any training in coach-driving, and controlling his six mouse colleagues (who had been turned into the coach's six horses), was extremely unsettling.

His situation was made worse as the coachman's livery in which he found himself was clearly not designed for him. It was tight around his groin and upper legs, restricting his movements, and this probably led to the summons he has received from the Fairyland police for dangerous driving on the way to the palace.

Mr Mouse had only just set out on the return journey shortly before midnight when, again, quoting from his letter: *"I was at last beginning to enjoy my new elevated position. Suddenly, there was another flash and bang, and I became a mouse again. Together with my six mates, I had a twenty mile walk home. And we had to carry this bloody great pumpkin too!*

If you are the person who placed Mr Mouse in the above situation, (without notification, prior training or the taking of proper body measurements, you are liable to prosecution under health and safety regulations.

Yours faithfully

Horace Windrush
Health & Safety Executive

Monseigneur Josephus Monteverdi
Chief Choirmaster - The Vatican Choir
The Piazza Venezia Cathedral
Vatican City   18th January, Anno Domini 1885

Dear Monseigneur Monteverdi,

We are writing to you in connection with your traditional practice of castrating your tenor choristers to enable them to achieve the 'High C' and other notes when performing those particular works.

Under new health and safety legislation, we would point out that this 'castrati' procedure is now illegal, (Section V, para IX, " Removal of healthy body parts to obtain additional skills or profit").

If you and other members of the Vatican Choir management wish to avoid prosecution, for any new tenor choristers you recruit this procedure must cease forthwith.

We recognise that our ruling will cause new choristers problems in achieving the very highest notes. So with the cooperation of a panel of volunteer test singers, we carried out some experiments using non-surgical means by which such notes might be reached. One of the most promising involved the singer sharply "clapping" his testicles between his palms at the moment he attempts the critical note. This worked, but the test singer was unable to carry out the action without dropping his music.

We also tried getting the singer to hold a large glass of ice cubes in front of his groin and to plunge his testicles into it at the appropriate moment. Again this worked, but it of course required him to be naked from the waist down, and we felt this might upset members of the congregation.

In spite of these failures, I am pleased to say that we then had a breakthrough. One of our senior executives is also a member of the Vatican Masonic Lodge. After studying the test failures he suggested that grasping the testicles using the unique Masonic handshake might achieve the desired result. And subsequent tests not only proved him correct but also shown that this can be carried out through the cassock fabric.

Those tests also showed that the 'angle of the approach' was critical for success. This means that individual chorister cannot achieve the required "squeeze" of his own testicles, but can successfully do so to the singer to his immediate right. (Our Masonic member says that is because, in the Masonic handshake, the thumb is on the outside of the grip).

You must therefore arrange for your new tenor choristers, (plus the individual chorister to the group's left), to both learn this handshake and to stand side-by-side while singing. A certain amount of practice, (plus complete trust in your neighbour's sense of timing and personal proclivities), will be vital.

Yours sincerely,

Thomaso Fettuccine

The Vatican Health and Safety Directorate

The Welsh Druids Association

First Floor, 24 Hazel Avenue, Wrexham, North Wales

Mr Owen Thomas
The Welsh Health and Safety Executive
The Rise, Clwyd,   5th August, Anno Domini 704

My dear Owen

I need to ask a favour. I wouldn't do so but it's a matter that threatens the very existence of our Druid movement here in North Wales. As you may know, the training to become a druid is lengthy, usually about twenty years. With inevitable drop-outs, the net result is that our Druid population is actually declining.

As if this wasn't bad enough, every Hallowe'en our leaders insist that we all traipse off to our sacred Hazel Grove at Llangollen and sacrifice fifty virgins! The blood involved, (so they say) fertilizes the soil and produces a good harvest the following year. It isn't rocket science to realise that more virgin sacrifices means fewer druid trainees!

As you know, Owen, as part of my druid responsibilities, I am our senior agronomist, and after last year's Hallowe'en sacrifices, I secretly did some tests. I set out two root vegetable plots and fertilised one plot with some of the virgins' blood and the other with guaranteed virgins' urine, (not easy to obtain) The results showed that the virgins' urine performed just as well as the blood! I have enclosed a bunch of carrots from the 'Urine' plot, which, are superb. (In my view the slightly astringent taste is a plus).

But you can imagine what a stodgy lot our Druid 'top brass' are! So I've been racking my brains for a way to persuade them to stop sacrificing virgins. I feel the only workable way would be if you could intervene to ban these sacrifices on health and safety grounds, and recommend the alternative virgins' urine treatment.

Changing over is perfectly workable. When Hallowe'en comes round we can hire fifty portable women's' toilets for the day. There will be two alternative toilet door notices, one saying "Women Fulfilled" and the other "Virgin Women".

Owen, the Welsh Druids may well be in jeopardy unless I can count on your help.

Yours, with best personal wishes,

David Llewellyn-Jones

Senior Druid and Chief Agronomist

Camden Health and Safety Directorate

London Borough of Camden Council, 23-28 Caledonian Road, London EC1 4SD

Miss Whiplash de Paris
Basement Flat
24 Fairfax Avenue
Kings Cross   18th November 1964

Dear Madam

We are advised that the above is your professional name, and that according to the voting register you are in fact Mrs Gladys Bolsworthy.

We understand from a Mr John Thomas that on Wednesday, 5th November inst, having not been invited to any firework parties, he responded to your "Roman Candle Massage Experience", as featured on your business card in a Kings Cross telephone box, and visited you.

According to Mr Thomas, during his consultation he sustained a number of small circular bruises he claimed were a result of your walking up and down his bare back and buttocks in your black leather boots with 7 inch stiletto heels while he was tied to your bed.

Clearly, from our perspective, this is a potentially dangerous activity. Having fully considered the matter, to protect the public you are in future required to use footwear more suited to the task. We would specify carpet slippers or plimsolls.

While this doesn't fall within our remit, Mr Thomas also claims that your "Oral Stimulation" treatment failed to improve his elocution as he expected, and may therefore be an offence under the Misrepresentation of Services Act.

Please acknowledge and confirm that you will take the above action.

Yours faithfully,

Julian Boulton

Health and Safety Manager

P.S. Our Chairman, Sir Percival Crabtree, has asked me to send his warm regards.

Westminster Health and Safety Executive

Third Floor, Thames View Buildings, 67-80 The Embankment, London

The Lord Chancellor
The House of Commons
Westminster

23rd May, 1344

Dear Lord Chancellor

You are aware of the unfortunate occurrence at the Grand Ball at Eltham Palace last month, when, as a result of the loss of her garter by Joan, Countess of Salisbury, His Majesty graciously establishing the Most Honourable Order of the Garter. And how impressive the ceremonial garter is, superbly decorated with gold thread, heavy beadwork and embroidery.

However, His Majesty's specification that the decoration be worn just below the left knee has unfortunately raised an important health and safety issue. From several complaints received, we have selected the following representative example. We quote from a letter from the private secretary to Lord Thomas de Beauchamps, as follows:-

"My Lord was attending the Garter service at St George's Chapel three weeks ago in his full regalia. My Lord is elderly and has very thin legs. So he instructed me to secure the Garter to his breeches with a safety pin, which I did".

From our health and safety perspective, this would appear to have been a sensible solution. But, again quoting from the secretary's letter:- *"However, as My Lord walked in the procession the weight of the garter began to exert a downward loading on his breeches. His full-length ermine cloak covered up his embarrassment, as nothing was seen to be amiss by those around him, and he was able to continue shuffling forward.*

All might have ended well. But when My Lord came to mounting the three steps to the Throne in order to kneel before King Edward, his trailing garter and breeches, (now round his ankles), caused My Lord to trip and and fall prostrate, causing severe bruising to his lower body. (The cloak continued to cover all, and the King assumed this was simply an act of abject fealty on My Lord's part".

This demonstrates that at present the wearing of the Garter below the knee can affect the health and safety of the wearer, (and possibly other important personages in close proximity). We would clearly not wish to go against His Majesty's specification as to the positioning of the Garter, and yet we have to prevent the risk of further injury.

So, as a result of tests we have carried out with the help of Lord Beauchamps, our ruling is that once the Garter has been attached to the lower left leg, it must be supported in the following manner. One end of a piece of stout string must be tied to it, and the other end carried up beneath the hose and chemise, diagonally across his upper body to his right armpit, and then down the sleeve to his right wrist, to which it must be attached.

While this may sound complicated, this particular positioning of the string provides two benefits; it not only prevents the Garter slipping down the leg, but the action of swinging the right arm forward when walking causes the person's left knee to be pulled forward. (As most of the Knights of the Order are elderly and find walking difficult, this would be a considerable benefit.)

Would you kindly confirm that you will pass these instructions on to all current and new Garter appointees.

Yours faithfully

William Makepiece

Health & Safety Director

Post Script: You might be amused to hear that having fitted the string in the above manner, Lord Beauchamps subsequently took the initiative of then attaching a corresponding string to his right calf with the other end taking a similar path to his left wrist. Then alternately swinging each arms, he was able to move his legs forward at an extremely pleasing rate, and this enabled him to catch his comely young maid of the bed-chamber for the first time in years.

City of London Health Directorate
Second Floor, Tudor House, The Thames Embankment, London

Mr Thos. Farriner
Farriner's Bakery
27-29 Pudding Lane
Cheapside   27th August, Year of our Lord, 1666

Dear Mr Farriner,

Thank you for your letter of the 15th August requesting permission to employ the services of the famous fire-breather, Mr Ignatius Pierpoint, to perform his "volcano" act at your Farriner Bakery Centenary Celebration. We understand this involves his taking mouthfuls of neat gin and then blowing them in vapour form in a five foot flaming column.

You state that you are planning his performance for the evening of the 1st September outside your premises in Pudding Lane before an invited audience of your customers, including the celebrated Mr Samuel Pepys, Secretary to the Admiralty.

Having examined the health and safety implications of your proposal fully, we have no objection to your employing Mr Pierpoint for your event. However, as you appreciate, Pudding Lane is close to the Thames, which means that at night the blustery winds off the river could affect Mr Pierpoint's control and direction of his "volcano" performance, possibly putting the health and safety of your visitors at risk.

So, in our view holding this performance outside is a health and safety risk to the public, and we therefore cannot give permission for this.

However, from our conversation, we understand that you would be prepared to adopt our directive and invite your customers into your bakery premises and hold Mr Pierpoint's performance inside, (where clearly there would be no wind problem). Subject to this, we would see no reason to withhold permission.

May we take this opportunity to wish your Centenary celebration every success. We look forward to hearing that on the night of the 1st September you lit up that part of our City!!

Yours sincerely,

Henry Puddleton

Senior Health and Safety Executive

Association of Scottish Clan Chieftains' Wives

Registered Office: 'Glen View', 23 The High Street, Inverness

Mr Hamish MacLeod
Scottish Health and Safety Directorate
23-27 The Parade, Glasgow   27th January 1493

Dear Mr MacLeod,

As you're aware, a growing number of our highland clan chiefs are adopting the new fashion garment called the 'Kilt' in place of the traditional trews. At our AGM last week, an emergency motion was passed, to draw your Directorate's attention to some serious Health and Safety issues concerning these 'Kilts'.

My members have become aware that while these 'Kilts' worn by our husbands not only look extremely stylish and dashing but also give full freedom of movement, they have one drawback - they also result in exposure of their wearers' genitalia to the elements at all times.

As a 'lowlander', you might not consider this important, but up here during the winter the constant, close proximity of the snow to our chiefs' private parts has led to total numbness of these organs, (and in the case of Chief Malcolm of the MacDonald clan, severe frostbite). Also, when our brave husbands are leading a battle charge, the abrasive damage that highland thistles can cause is horrendous. Many of our husbands now have no interest in, (nor are capable of), sexual relations. In some instances the cold and pain have been so intense that they have suffered memory-loss about the whole subject!

We have studied H & S regulations, and we believe we have a case against our husbands, under section 34, para 23: **'Subjecting personal appendages to stress or damage of a nature likely to cause loss of their principal function'.** Flora McGonigal, our legal adviser (and, incidentally a part-time butcher), has suggested that section 6, para 14 might also apply: **"Attempting 'passing off', i.e. seeking to offer frozen meat as fresh".**

My committee and I look forward to hearing from you.

Yours faithfully

Moira McTavish

Secretary A.S.C.C.W.

Greater London Health & Safety Executive

Health and Safety House, 27-35 Thamesmead House, High Holborn, London

Sir Henry Bunkington, *Bart C.H.*
Postmaster General
380-400 Piccadilly, London   28th September 1979

Dear Sir Henry,

      May I draw your attention to what has been exposed as a potentially dangerous risk to your postal operatives.

      On Friday, 5th September, operative Gerald Smith, was in the process of delivering an envelope to 85 year old pensioner, Mrs Ariadne Biggins, at 13 The Buildings, Canning Town. Arriving at her door, postman Smith raised his postbag toward his face in order to identify the relevant envelope. In doing so, the letter initially snagged on the lip of his bag, and, as it came free, the corner of the sharp 90 degree-cornered envelope penetrated his left nostril, causing a small nose bleed. Unfortunately a few drops of blood fell onto Mrs Biggins's envelope as he pushed it through her letterbox.

      In fact, the white envelope contained a birthday greetings card. As postman Smith subsequently pointed out, had the envelope been coloured red, (as with many greetings cards), the bloodstains would have gone unnoticed. As it was, Mrs Biggins, being of a nervous disposition, assumed that her husband, centenarian Percy Smith, had been abducted, and that the blood-stained envelope contained (a small) part of her husband's body with a ransom demand, and she called the Police.

      Clearly, traditional 90 degree envelope corners represent a risk to postal operatives, and we have tested alternative delivery methods. One of the most promising was shown to be the 'snorkel' type face-mask which fully protects the operative's eyes, nose and mouth. Regrettably some postmen participating in the trial took things unnecessarily far by also using breathing tubes with their face-masks, and several elderly Canning Town residents became distressed, assuming that the Thames had flooded at Wapping.

After consideration, the Executive has decided that the best solution will be for the traditional four-cornered envelope to be replaced with a <u>circular</u> version. As easy to carry as the traditional envelope, this shape would totally avoid the risk of sharp corners entering any of your members' orifices while fulfilling their duties.

Would you kindly make the necessary arrangement with the Stationery Office.

Yours faithfully

Gerald Spindletrees

Health & Safety Executive

British Empire Health and Safety Directorate

The Foreign Office, Parliament Square, London, Great Britain

Mr Mustapha Karzi
Deputy Chief Castrator
The Sultan's Topkapi Palace
Istanbul

12th December 1892

Dear Mr Karzi

On behalf of the Directorate and the British Government, I am writing to you concerning one of your junior castrators, Mr Terrence Todger, of 3 The Medina, Istanbul. As you may know, Mr Todger is an English national, and therefore protected under the British Empire 'Health and Safety at Work in Foreign Parts' regulations.

He has contacted us regarding a very painful injury he sustained at work on the 31st October, while carrying out his duties. As we understand it, Mr Todger was preparing to operate on a member of the public who had applied for employment in the harem and, (appreciating the castration requirement), the person had been happily sedated with hashish ready for the procedure.

Using what we understand to be your traditional "two house bricks" castration method, Mr Todger grasped the two bricks, extended both arms to their maximum width, and then brought the bricks sharply together. While the resulting castration was a complete success for the harem applicant, unfortunately in the process Mr Todger caught his right index finger between the bricks, causing a fracture of the intermediate phalange.

From a health and safety aspect, our research team have considered several options to protect our nationals from this sort of injury. We have decided that any British operatives in your employ must cease using the present "bricks" procedure, and instead adopt a new British invention called the 'nutcracker', (some samples enclosed). Not only will you find this instrument considerably more efficient than your present method, but we would also point out that it can be operated with one hand, and will therefore double your productivity.

Please confirm your acceptance of this ruling by return.

Yours faithfully,

Rupert Chamberlain

Health and Safety in the Empire

Judea Health & Safety Directorate

24 Mount of Olives Avenue, Jerusalem, Judea

Your Majesty King Balthasar
The Royal Palace
Saba, Persia   17th January, Anno Domini 1

Majesty, greetings,

We have heard from a Mr Joseph of The Stables, Donkey and Manger Inn, Nazareth, regarding the birthday gifts you and your colleague, King Caspar of Tharsis, gave Mr Joseph's newly born son on the 25th last.

Mr Joseph points out that, while your gifts for his son were extremely generous, he is concerned about possible health risks. Having looked into the matter we concur.

Your gift of Frankincense, while usually harmless to adults, can cause breathing problems in the very young. And the gift of Myrrh by your colleague, King Caspar, (to whom we are writing separately), is listed under the 'Dangerous Substances' Regulations. It is an embalming oil. Applied to newly-born babies' skins, it can trigger exczema.

Mr Joseph tells us that he and his wife found the Gold from your colleague, King Melchior, very handy, and the family plan to use the money to open a chain of carpentry outlets for their son to manage.

We appreciate that when the star rose, you and your colleagues felt you had to leave immediately and follow it. So, presumably you had little time to select gifts. But from a heath and safety viewpoint, better choices might have been a toy camel or teddy bear, both available from the Saba supermarket, (which was open till midnight on Christmas Eve).

Yours respectfully,

Solomon Isiah
Health & Safety Executive

The Royal Court of King Cetshwayo

The King's Kraal of Ten Thousand Cattle, Rorke's Drift View, Isandlwana

The Hon. Charles de Vere Fortescue
British Overseas Health & Safety Directorate
23 Pall Mall, London   24th March 1879

My dear Pongo,

   May I firstly say what an absolute hoot it was to have studied with you at Oxford. (Did you realise that I'm the first Zulu to take a degree in medicine. Cool eh?)

   As you know, following our end-of-term leaving party two weeks ago, (when you danced on the Don's dining table without your togs), I have now arrived back at my father's kraal at Isandlwana. So I missed taking part in the Rorke's Drift battle on the 22nd – 23rd of January against your British army, that you'll have read about in 'The Times'

   Now, Pongo, old chum, to get down to 'brass pins', as you English say. I accept that we had over 3,500 more bods at Rorke's Drift than you did, and there's no doubt your chaps must have fought most bravely to have won the battle. So you may feel I'm being a stinker, but I'm afraid I've got bad news.

   One of the key English characteristics I learned at Oxford was 'always playing with a straight bat'. I'm therefore writing on health and safety grounds to draw your attention to the insidious and underhanded behaviour of your British commanding officer, a Lieutenant Chard, in ordering his troops to wear their white pith helmets for the battle. As nothing on the veldt is absolutely white, our brave impis could have had no idea of the damage the fierce sun's rays, reflecting off the white helmets, was doing to their eyesight.

   It was only during our witch doctor's sick parade following the battle that this became clear. For your information the list that morning was :- bullet wounds 773, bayonet wounds 234, concussion 123, broken limbs 97, sprains 53, diarrhoea 693, and eye strain 2,879.

So you can see just how serious this matter is. Your Queen Victoria would be horrified if she knew about such underhand and dastardly behaviour by her army. It simply isn't cricket!

Now, Pongo, I think I've also come up with the solution! Another thing I learned about the English at Oxford was the importance of 'tea'. As it happens, at the battle of Isandlwana a week before Rorke's Drift, we captured a huge amount of English tea. As so many of your soldiers drink it, our impis thought it must bestow magical fighting powers on the drinker, but all it did was to cause extensive diarrhoea, (see sick parade list above).

However, what we discovered by chance was that your tea could be used successfully to dye the English pith helmets. Do you remember that bumptious little swot, Bodger Grey, in the third year? Well, using his family's brand of tea, the helmets ended up a very pleasant khaki hue.

From a health and safety perspective, may I ask that you take up this complaint (and suggested solution) with your British Army High Command, and ensure that in future battles our impis are not exposed to this insidious practice.

With very best personal regards, old chum,

Rupert Cetshwayo

Chief's No 1 Son

*By the way, I gather 'Bodger' is now an Earl. What a hoot!

Cardiff Ballet Company

Mr Ifor Rees-Williams
Glamorgan Health and Safety Directorate
27-29 High Street
Cardiff, Glamorgan CC23 8ER   4th September 2004

Dear Mr Rees-Williams

I refer to the accident that befell a member of our chorus, Miss Myfanwy Roberts, three weeks ago when she landed badly while practising her 'Jeté' and sustained a bruised big toe. This was during the rehearsals for our first performance of "Swan Lake", as part of Welsh Centenary celebrations.

Following your subsequent health and safety investigation, I am writing to say that we have fully adopted your directive that all our dancers' ballet shoes should be fitted with protective steel toecaps. (The conversion work was carried out by Ewan Jones Ltd, manufacturers of miners' safety boots, here in Cardiff.)

While it is undeniably true that we have not had a foot injury of any kind since adopting the new toecaps, last night's première of our "Swan Lake" at the Cardiff Municipal Hall proved less than an unqualified success. I quote from the Cardiff Echo arts correspondent's review in today's paper.

"In act two, when the Swan Queen (Mrs Gladys Williams) performed her solo 'entrechat', (the movement whereby she springs into the air rapidly crossing her legs several times), there was a loud ringing noise that had several people in the audience reaching for their mobile phones.

In performing their solo in act four, the twenty little cygnets caused a loud vibration and creaking of the elderly Municipal stage. I thought swans were meant to be mute, but with this noisy flock it was more like a 'Duck Pond' than a 'Swan Lake'. While I would recommend Echo readers to see the ballet, take some earplugs, (and leave mobile phones at home)".

While we adopted your directive in good faith, we submit that it destroys the whole essence of our art, and ask that you reconsider the matter, particularly when I tell you that Miss Roberts, who suffered the accident in the first place, now admits that her boyfriend has a foot fetish and probably caused her bruised toe!

Yours faithfully

Lance Crumble

Chief Choreographer

BELFRIDGES DEPARTMENT STORE

287-320 OXFORD STREET, LONDON W1

Miss Doris Smith
2a Borrit Road
Shepherds Bush, London   5th April 1885

Dear Miss Smith

I regret to have to notify you that your employment as a junior window dresser with Belfridges is terminated forthwith. Please collect your effects and leave today.

Since you started here, you've carried out your duties responsibly. This is with the exception of the unfortunate situation three nights ago concerning the new lifelike wax mannequins we've begun incorporating into our window displays. On that occasion, in the late evening you had worked on your own in the window and had assembled five female mannequins in our main window ready for dressing the following morning.

While I appreciate that, in career terms, you ultimately want to get into show business, having completed the mannequins assembly, your subsequent action in removing your own clothes and posing with them in the window was reprehensible. Had you remained totally still, even this might have gone unnoticed by the passing traffic. Unfortunately, you then decided to perform your somewhat exotic 'dance of spring'.

As you must have seen, a large crowd immediately collected outside our window. In itself this didn't represent a problem, (in fact the directors were delighted!) However, the Westminster Health and Safety Directorate have written to us pointing out that your actions also caused the horses of a passing omnibus to shy and bolt, throwing the conductor from the alighting platform, and causing pregnant Mrs Gladys Brown, sitting on the upper deck, to break her waters.

The Westminster Health and Safety Directorate has pointed out that no public entertainment may put the safety of the public at risk. However, they appreciate that it was a one-off occurrence and, providing we act responsibly in terminating your employment, they will take no further action.

Yours faithfully,

Percival Privett

Personnel Manager

Post Script: If you would like to leave matters for a month or two 'for the dust to settle', and then reapply for employment, we will be happy immediately to offer you the position of senior window dresser.

South London Health and Safety Executive

Council Chambers, The Butterworth Centre, Lewisham, South London

Mr Algernon Twist
3 Station Road
Lewisham, South London   2nd February 1885

STRICTLY CONFIDENTIAL

Dear Mr Twist

I am sorry to write to you on this painful matter, but since you have moved into the area, your wife's presence has unfortunately caused problems that, we feel, jeopardise the health and safety of the Lewisham public.

We do not seek to criticise your wife because of her extraordinarily plain appearance, although we note that she won the South London 'Ugliest Wife of the Year' award a month ago, (for which, incidentally, many congratulations). However, when she is out in our local community, her appearance has unfortunately caused a number of problems, of which the following are examples:

•Two weeks ago, while driving his hay wagon through Lewisham village, Mr Henry Troop was mesmerised by your wife, and collided with The Hon. George Figgis's brougham. Lady Figgis was deposited on the floor of the coach, breaking her lorgnettes.

•Last Friday, on catching sight of your wife in Market Street, Constable Dumbledon, accidentally walked into the village gibbet, sustaining concussion and a black eye.

•Yesterday, while on his ladder cleaning the upper Town Hall windows, Mr Digby Brown caught sight of your wife on the pavement below and dropped his bucket. Unfortunately the Mayor was leaving the building at the time, and his regalia were soaked.

To protect the Lewisham public from such risks, we must insist that your wife may only be away from your residence between the hours of 11pm and 5am, (with the exception of Hallowe'en night, of course).

We appreciate that this is an extremely onerous ruling, and we are pleased to be able to offer the following exception. We have been in contact with Lewisham's leading beauty salon. They have generously agreed to offer your wife a paid position walking round the village wearing their sandwich board with a 'before' and 'after' message about their beautifying services. As part of payment, they are also prepared to offer your wife a weekly beauty treatment, providing she is happy to wait til late evening to visit the salon.

We hope this is acceptable to you and your wife.

Once again, please accept our apologies for having to instigate this ruling. But bear in mind that at least something good has come out of this for you and your neighbours. Since you moved to Station Road, the pigeon flock that had been roosting there and causing such a mess with their droppings have been scared away.

Yours faithfully,

Gilbert Runcible

Health and Safety Executive

South London Health and Safety Executive
Safety House, The High Street, Clapham, South London CL12 3DT

Mr George Smith - Proprietor
The Corner Garage & Tyre Centre
67-70 Station Road
New Cross, London SE12 4DR

28th July 1992

Dear Mr Smith

We are of course aware of the fast-growing popularity of female breast enhancement, not only for dancers and other professional entertainers, but also among the general public.

We note that you have introduced a **"Ten Minute Boob Inflation Service"** at your garage. We understand this simply involves fitting a small valve to the underside of each female customer's breasts and then inflating them with your garage air line. I am writing to advise you that this service conflicts with Health and Safety regulations. This is supported by complaints we have received from a number of women about problems encountered after receiving your service. These include the following representative cases :-

Mrs Ariadne Heliotrope-Fisher, a professional opera singer, was halfway through her 'Mimi' aria at the Festival Hall when she realised her left breast was slowly losing air. Fortunately she had the presence of mind to rest her deflating breast on her music stand for the rest of the performance, and only the conductor and the first violinist noticed.

Mrs Delphine Forsdyke was forced to resign her captaincy of the Surbiton synchronised swimming team because, after your service, she was unable to get below the pool surface.

Miss Annemarie Polder, a masseuse professionally known as 'Miss Whiplash from Amsterdam', left a client lying on her bed while she commenced her 'Flying Dutchperson' act, launching herself from her mantelpiece intending to land on him. However, her breasts were clearly over-inflated, because she bounced off the bed and out of her bedroom window. Her client has refused to pay for her services.

While we do not wish to ban your "Ten Minute Boob Inflation Service", to avoid the above problems you must adopt the following health and safety directive. You must offer a Fourteen Day 'Free Adjustment' Period, whereby customers experiencing problems can return and have their pressure levels adjusted, free of charge. Also you must employ a responsible person to be your 'breast pressure adjustment operative'.

Yours faithfully,

Algernon Prickle
Health and Safety Executive

P.S. Mr Smith, I'm a responsible person and I'm not particularly happy at the HSE. So I was wondering whether I could apply for the above position?

The Earl Leofric of Mercia
The Manor, Coventry

14th May Anno Domini 1035

Dear Sir Leofric

I apologise for troubling you. However, a health and safety matter has arisen concerning your wife, the Lady Godgifu.

You will know that on this coming Sunday, 5th August at noon, she plans to ride entirely naked through the main streets of Coventry, to show support for the town's peasants protesting again your Lordship's taxes. We understand that Her Ladyship has notified all the peasants living along her proposed route, and has demanded that they keep their shutters closed as she passes, (including the well-known voyeur, Mr P. Tom, a tailor residing at 4, The Street, South Coventry).

As you appreciate, health and safety regulations also cover self-harm, particularly for a person of the rank of Her Ladyship. There are three areas :-

* Firstly, as we understand it, the horse she will ride stands over 18 hands. With effect from 1st January 1032, for a horse of this height it is now necessary for the rider to wear a safety hat, (even though, regrettably, in her case this will partially cover her renowned, blond hair).

* Secondly, riding a stirruped horse of this height barefoot is now banned. She will need to wear at least light plimsolls to protect her feet.

* Thirdly, a somewhat sensitive matter. Even with her horse walking at a slow pace over the distance involved, the chafing effect of the saddle on Her Ladyship's naked buttocks is a further concern. A solution suggested by our senior director, (who's an avid fan), is that her hair which naturally falls to her knees can be coiled to form a protective 'seat' for the journey.

Will you be please ensure that Her Ladyship adopts these directives.

Yours faithfully

Robin Loxley

Health & Safety Director

P.S. Incidentally, we've kept Mr Tom under observation, and the only suspicious activity is that he has been out and purchased a large drill.

West Carmarthen Cathedral

Cathedral Close, High Street, Llandysul, Carmarthenshire, Wales

Mr Bryn Thomas
Wales Health & Safety Directorate
The Parade,
Llandysul, Carmarthenshire

16th November 1997

Dear Mr Thomas

As choirmaster I am responding to your letter of the 12th November.

Let me first point out that we have made tremendous strides in attracting larger attendances at the cathedral, particularly by introducing new and challenging works for our choir. Last Sunday's performance, (to which your letter refers), was an important occasion in that we were introducing a new version of the 'Hallelujah Chorus', adapted by Owen Wynn-Thomas, as a choir solo.

One of the distinctive ways in which the singing of this version differs from the original is that the "hah" and "yah" syllables at the beginning and end of the word "Hallelujah" are greatly extended, each lasting up to five seconds. As part of the choreography, Mr Wynn-Thomas had also specified that at this point the choir's faces need to be turned symbolically to Heaven.

In hindsight, it was perhaps unfortunate timing that during one of these extended "hahs" the cathedral bells started their first peal. Probably disturbed by the vibration, a quantity of dust and pigeon droppings, accumulated on the high beams, was dislodged and fell directly into the open mouths of the choir below. This caused much coughing and choking, and the solo had to be abandoned. Mrs Gladys Jones, contralto, fainted and was escorted to the vestry where several glasses of communion wine were needed to revive her.

As you point out, from a health and safety viewpoint, we should urgently consider ways of reducing the amount of 'risk time', i.e. the time our choir have their mouths wide open during their recital. In this connection your advice is that when we sing choral words like "Hallelujah" we should change the "a" sound to a "oo" sound. Thus for example, "Hallelujah" would be sung as "Hoollelooyooh". You calculate that this will reduce the 'risk' time from thirty-five to twelve seconds.

We are prepared to accept your ruling for this particular piece. However, we will shortly be starting rehearsals for our popular Christmas Carol service, and I do not feel the Bishop or our congregation will be happy if we sing such selections as "Ding doong merrily on hoo", "Hook the Hooralds angels soong" or "Awoo in a moonger".

Yours faithfully

Julian Glendower

J.D. Glendower – Choirmaster

Greater London Health and Safety Directorate

Council Offices, 201-207 Praed Street, Paddington, London W14 7DR

Mr G. Fawkes
14 Cable Street
Stepney, East London   2nd November, year of our Lord 1605

Dear Mr Fawkes,

We are writing concerning your recent purchase and collection of 2 tonnes of gunpowder from the Woolwich Arsenal, and your stated purpose for this material. We would make the following points:-

On your purchase order, you stated that the material is required for "the demolition of defunct Protest edifices". Please clarify this.

We note that you have varied the above gunpowder by adding Saltpetre to increase its strength, and we acknowledge receipt of the sample you submitted to us on the 27th ultimate.

We have completed the tests to determine its new strength. (These are standard tests for all explosive powders which include curry, snuff, laxative and cocaine).

In this instance unfortunately we had an in-house 'glitch' in that your sample was miss-labelled 'snuff 'rather than gunpowder. After sampling, our chief analyst, who happens to be a regular snuff user, recorded the off-the-cuff comment that your sample 'nearly blew his hat off'. (I shouldn't be telling you this, but our chief analyst is a cantankerous old goat who gives us juniors at the GLHSD a lot of stick, and we had a laugh about what might have happened if your sample had been labelled 'laxative'!)

Regarding the storage of this material, your decision to use a cold, damp location is fully in line with our 'Storage of Explosive Materials' regulations, and your choice of the cellars of the House of Lords at Westminster seems eminently sensible. However, there is a potential problem.

As you may be aware, the official Opening of Parliament will take place at Westminster on the 5th inst, to be attended by His Gracious Majesty King James. So it's essential that the delivery and storage of your material is fully completed <u>no later than midnight on the 4th November</u>, so that there will be no risk of disrupting the ceremony.

Yours faithfully,

George Thackary

Junior Health and Safety Executive

Greater London Health and Safety Directorate

Council Offices, 201-207 Praed Street, Paddington, London W14 7DR

Mr G. Fawkes
Cell 3, West Wing
The Tower of London
Tower Hill   8th November, the year of our Lord 1605

Dear Mr Fawkes,

We are concerned that we have not received an acknowledgement of our letter of the 2nd inst, and I have had a lot of trouble locating your new address at the Tower. An immediate reply is required for our records.

On a lighter note, following the Westminster Gazette's coverage of our involvement in your case, you may not realise that you've become something of a celebrity. So far, we've received over 50 congratulatory letters addressed to you. Many of them are from wives of the Members of the House of Lords offering you financial inducements to repeat your activities.

This is obviously when you are up and about again. We will post these letters and payments on to you.

Yours faithfully,

George Thackary

Junior Health and Safety Executive

EAST LONDON HEALTH AND SAFETY EXECUTIVE
HEALTH HOUSE, 57-59 OXFORD STREET, LONDON W2

Monsieur Antoine Beauclair
Proprietor - 'Le Grand Crapaud'
23 Tottenham Court Road , London E1   10th May, 1935

Dear Monsieur Beauclair

May we wish you 'bonne chance' with your splendid achievement in opening one of the first French restaurants in London recently. Our role is to protect the health and safety interests of English persons. As part of that responsibility, one of our inspectors has carried out our normal ('mystery shopper') visit to 'Le Grand Crapaud' to determine whether our nationals are at any risk in your premises.

Your efforts to provide, in English, not only your menus but also your general signage is admirable. While most signs passed our health and safety regulations with flying colours, those in your men's urinal and men's/ ladies' lavatories require some attention. Your following wording needs to be changed :-

In the men's urinal :- *"Wherever possible stand with a full erection while urinating, and keep good control of your hose. Otherwise your outpouring could tumble onto the floor and cause dangerous skating".*

"The management cannot be responsible if you bend over our pissoir to urinate and sink your dentures into our bottom. Monocles and bicycles may also be sunk without recompense".

"On completion, gentlemen must recapture all the flies they have let loose before leaving the kiosk, in order not to frighten the fillies".

In the men's and ladies' lavatories :- *"To flush, employ the chain softly. Excessive force could encourage our cistern to descend, possibly striking your head and causing conception. And if the paper is no more, please use your moustache to wipe the seat before exiting".*

Please have the above signs changed with immediate effect.

Yours faithfully,

Wilfred Goodbody

Junior Health and Safety Executive

East London Health and Safety Directorate

Health & Safety House, 24 Mile End Road, Bermondsey, London

Mr George Smith
Manager - Council Cleansing Department
Westminster Borough Council
289-322 Waterloo Road, London   12th September, Year of our Lord, 1837

Dear Mr Smith

I am writing to you regarding your Council's recent installation of the newly invented silvered-glass mirrors in your public lavatory at Barbican Road, Rotherhythe.

While we endorse your progressive thinking in being the first Council in East London to adopt this recent invention as a benefit for the local populace, it is important to appreciate that most members of the public using that facility are unused to mirrors in public lavatories. So it is perhaps unfortunate that your Council chose to install these at head height directly above the trough in the men's urinal.

I have to point out that this has resulted in health and safety aspects being infringed. In this connection we have received a significant number of complaints about these mirrors from users of your facility. Here are two representative examples:-

a)   While urinating, Mr Harry Thomas of 23 Tides Reach, Greenwich, took a step forward   to inspect a boil on his nose, and in doing so put his right foot down the trough. As a result he not only lost his shoe but also broke his toe.

b)   Mr Tom Jones of 14 Thames Lane, Wapping, was apparently mesmerised by his image in the mirror and proceeded to urinate over the leg (and dog) of Mr William Bottle standing beside him. Fortunately Mr Bottle had lost his lower right leg at Balaclava and has a wooden one, so the effect of the dowsing was not apparent to him until several days later when his leg began to show signs of wet rot. (Incidentally Mr Bottle's dog developed a nasty case of mange).

As the above cases demonstrate, it is clearly dangerous to position these mirrors where the Council has done so. On health and safety grounds you are therefore required to have them re-sited with immediate effect.

Yours faithfully

Lancelot Dripping

Health and Safety Inspector

His Majesty Prasutagus,
King of the Iceni Celts,
The Fortified Encampment
Long Stratton
Angle Land

Juno XV11, Anno Domini 60

Majesty, greetings,

We are writing to you on a matter concerning your wife, the Lady Boudicca, (as we do not recognise female royal persons in our conquered territories). While we understand that you are semi-retired, you nevertheless have a statutory Heath and Safety responsibility for the activities of your family.

We have received a report from Mr Caius Paulinus, commander of the 3rd Roman army, whose legions your wife, her daughters and the Iceni tribe annihilated at Camulodunum two weeks ago.

Having escaped with his life, but understandably traumatised by his ordeal, Mr Paulinus described your wife Boudicca in his report as follows:- "Supported by her two loud-mouthed daughters who richly deserved the deflowering they had been given, this frightening celtish witch, with huge red hair and breasts to match, adopted battle practices against my men that defy the imagination of civilised races".

Having studied his report in full, but wishing to maintain a balanced view, we see no contravention of health and safety regulations in the majority of methods by which Lady Boudicca achieved the above victory; including garrotting, disembowelling, hanging, dismemberment, nose removal and anal staking. However, as reported by Mr Paulinus, your wife has also adopted the horrifying practice of fitting large, dangerous scythes to her war chariots' wheel hubs. Positioned two cubits above ground level, in battle these can cause severe damage to the manhood of our legionaires.

This practice contravenes Health and Safety regulation 305, Section 8 ("Circumcision or castration without prior warning, anaesthetic or doctor's letter.")

In the event that Lady Boudicca will not agree to discontinue fitting these scythes, to avoid prosecution before each battle she must ensure that protective sheepskin sleeves are fitted over each blade, which should limit the health and safety risk to no more than bruising.

Please acknowledge your acceptance of these instructions.

Yours faithfully

Marcus Silvanus

Health & Safety Directorate

South Dorset Health and Safety Directorate

23-27 Willington Parade, The Limes, Bournemouth, Dorset DD3 2HY

The Manager – Council Cleansing Department
Dorset County Council
258 – 279 London Road
Dorchester DR12 3WE   3rd January 2001

Dear Sir or Madam,

Following an interview with Mr and Mrs Reginald Bostick of 'Shangri-La', 23 Cliff View, Bournemouth, we are writing to you regarding a health and safety issue concerning your public toilet at the corner of Hazel Grove and Vicarage Drive, Bournemouth, which we understand is the first in the town to be fitted with automatic self-sanitizing toilet seats.

On 16th December last, Mr and Mrs Bostick were out Christmas shopping in The Parade. Half way through the morning Mr Bostick found he needed to use a public toilet. While there were two facilities close at hand, the Bosticks walked several hundred yards to your Hazel Grove toilet because Mr Bostick was nervous about using standard toilet facilities. (His brother apparently caught an unpleasant rash from a public toilet seat in Kuala Lumpur during the war).

While his wife waited outside with the shopping, Mr Bostick entered one of the cubicles and sat down on the seat to carry out his evacuation. Clearly your toilet then malfunctioned, because, as Mr Bostick described in his own words:

"I had hardly got started when a buzzer sounded and the seat began to revolve. Fortunately, as an ex-commando, I have fast reactions and I had the presence of mind to quickly lift my feet onto the seat as it continued to revolve. It had turned about 180 degrees and I was facing the toilet wall when I spotted and pressed an emergency stop button.

My trousers had got entangled with the seat, and I had great difficulty in moving. So I had to complete my business in this position".

As if this wasn't sufficiently disconcerting, before he could then extricate himself from your toilet, Mr Bostick's buttocks were sprayed with a strong disinfectant from beneath the seat, causing an unpleasant stinging sensation. As Mr Bostick said, *"At that moment my brother's experience flashed before my eyes."*.

As we understand it, had the seat completed its full programme, Mr Bostick's genital area would also have been scoured with a heavy-duty wire brush, and then subjected to a blast of extremely hot air.

Having fully considered this unfortunate case, we feel immediate steps need to be taken by the Council to protect Bournemouth residents.

Firstly, we require you to fit emergency stop buttons in prominent, easy to reach positions, and secondly, to put posters up on all walls of the facility with instructions on what to do in the event of a seat malfunction.

Secondly, to protect your Council from legal action, these instructions must also be printed on each sheet of toilet paper in the cubicles, one of which the evacuator must sign to indicate that he or she has read and understood the instructions. On leaving the facility the signed sheet must be posted (reply paid) to your Council offices.

Please acknowledge this directive and take the required action.

Yours faithfully,

Lance Todmarsh

Health and Safety Directorate

Inverness Health and Safety Executive
The Council Offices, 78-83 Rob Roy Parade, Inverness

His Royal Highness Prince Charles Edward Stuart
Commander in Chief, The Highlander Army
Culloden Moor, Near Inverness

18th April, Year of our Lord 1746

Highness,

As loyal Scots, may we firstly express our condolences about the unfortunate rout of your highland troops by the English at the Culloden battle last Wednesday.

However the main reason for contacting you is that we have received a letter from one of your highlanders, a Mr William McTavish of the Fraser clan, which we feel raises an important health and safety issue that will affect all of your future battles.

At Culloden it is true that your highlanders had to charge some 200 yards over marshy ground to engage the English troops. However this doesn't explains their state of extreme distress and debility when they finally reached the English lines. It seems that many of your highlanders hardly had the strength to wield their claymores.

Mr McTavish has perhaps provided the explanation by pointed out that, as kilts have no pockets, he and his colleagues have to carry all their worldly goods in their sporrans. (In Mr McTavish's case, on the day of the battle his sporran contained a pipe and baccy, two chicken legs, his flint and tinder box, a lump of bread, two Fraserborough kippers, and his false teeth). Together with the metal studs and bead decoration on the sporran itself, the overall weight was substantial.

This weight was hanging immediately in front of Mr McTavish's genitals. During normal ambulation, this would not have any debilitating effect, but when he charged, a pendulous rhythm began, with his sporran fetching his genitals a blow at every stride. According to Mr McTavish, after the 200 yard charge, his lower body felt numb and he was more concerned with holding his genitals than his claymore. Clearly, this applied to the whole highlander army and was the cause of their distress.

Highness, I am therefore writing to say that your army must in future meet health and safety regulations on this matter. This means that for any future charges, while your men will obviously hold their claymores in one hand, to prevent the above painful impacting you must instruct them to carry their sporrans in their other hand.

Perhaps you would kindly confirm your agreement to the above directive.

Yours faithfully

Hamish McIntosh

Health & Safety Director

St Paul's Residential Care Home

238-240 Thames Reach, The Embankment, London

The Chief Executive
London Health and Safety Executive
23-28 Fleet Street, London   8th November 1964

Dear Sir or Madam

As you may know, the first shop selling the new American 'Doughnuts' recently opened near us at 23, Ludgate Circus. As a special treat for one of our senior residents, cathedral ex-warden Mr Henry Thompson, (whose 90th birthday we were planning to celebrate), we sent out especially for one of these new 'doughnuts' for his party.

We chose one of the round variety that had been injected with a jam filling and generously sprinkled with colourful "Hundreds and Thousands". When it arrived it really looked wonderful. It was a particularly cold day, and in the absence of any preparation instructions, our cook heated the doughnut in the oven. We then ceremonially brought it out in the middle of the party, placed it in front of Mr Thompson and stuck a single lighted candle in it, to the accompaniment of "Happy Birthday" by the staff and residents.

In hindsight, perhaps it was the piercing by the candle holder, but half way through the singing there was a muffled bang and the doughnut exploded, with the "Hundreds and Thousands" flying in all directions. Mr Thompson, a first world war veteran, momentarily thought he was back in the trenches, and dived under Lady Winkleman's blanket. While the dough caused no harm to the residents, the tiny droplets of jam landing on exposed flesh gave some of our more nervous members the impression that they had caught something terminal. Surprisingly, the 'Hundreds and Thousands' caused actual damage. These tiny sugar pieces, projected at high speed, shredded Mr Thompson hairpiece, and cracked his Royal Dalton chamber pot.

While Lady Winkleman has invited Mr Thompson to repeat his actions whenever the mood takes him, it is clear that these new doughnuts are dangerous. Can you therefore please take up this matter with The Doughnut Centre at Ludgate Circus.

Yours faithfully

Guinevere Bolsworthy (Matron)

City of London Health Directorate

Second Floor, Tudor House, Thames Embankment, London

Oliver Charles Cromwell, Esquire
First Lord Protector of England, Scotland and Ireland
Clerkenwell Close, London   21st April, 1653

My Lord Protector,

Please accept our respectful congratulations for your decisive action in taking over Parliament yesterday. Throwing down the Royal Mace and your stirring words, "Gentlemen, you have sat too long for any good you have been doing lately", were an inspiration to all. And when you left the House and addressed the several thousand of us waiting outside, your Lordship made a stirring and imposing figure.

The only risk, of course, with such public appearances is that the 'hoi polloi' are given the opportunity to see your personal mannerisms, which they naturally emulate. So it's unfortunate that at the end of your speech, (while you were still in public view), you chose to pick your nose.

Our medical specialist has pointed out that, if undertaken with excessive enthusiasm, this habit can lead to over-penetration of the nasal cavities, and result in swellings and exterior facial protuberances on the upper part of the nostril. This clearly happened in your case, and the resulting bulge on the side of your nose has erroneously become known as your 'wart'. When you commissioned Peter Lely, to paint your portrait "warts and all", we assume you prevailed on him to move your protuberance to your chin. And how much better it looks there!

However, we are writing respectfully to point out to your Lordship that this nose-picking habit of yours is contrary to Health and Safety Regulation (1653), specifically Section 243, para 7, "Excessive probing of human orifices for gain or profit".

Unfortunately the huge number of members of the public who were present during your speech and who saw your action have decided that nose-picking is now the social thing to do - a major additional workload of health and safety prosecutions for us. So may we respectfully ask your Lordship that when in the public gaze, you refrain from carrying out this unfortunate habit.

Yours sincerely,

William Fortescue-Stalybrass
Senior Health and Safety Executive

Sunshine Home for Retired Circus Performers

Sunshine House, 67-74 Cliff Parade, Bournemouth, Dorset

Henry Crimple Esq.
Chief Health and Safety Officer
Dorset County Council
27-35 The High Street
Bournemouth, Dorset   16th September 1964

Dear Mr Crimple,

As matron of the above establishment, I am writing to tell you that many of our septuagenarian members were astonished and disturbed to receive your health and safety directive of the 9th September regarding sex for persons of this age group.

Your directive states that "because of the high incidence of worn hips and knees at this age, coitus must be carried out slowly, calmly, and with these major joints at rest. Apart from the removal of garments, to minimise excessive flexing of these joints, the union should only be undertaken with both parties lying full-length".

With respect, many of our older members enjoy highly imaginative unions. For example:-

1.Mr Hector Spencer, an ex-trapeze artist, enjoys swinging on his bedroom chandelier and executing a double loop before touching down on his friend, Mrs Ariadne Phillips. Commented Mrs Phillips, 'while Hector's death-defying decent is from over 12 feet, his arrival is like thistledown'. At that moment the risk of an arthritic twinge is hardly uppermost in our minds!'

2.Russian-born Mr and Mrs Ivanov, previously well-known in the entertainment world as 'The Siberian Bendy Ben and Barbie', squeeze themselves into Sunshine Home's 5ft by 4 ft kitchen refrigerator for their weekly coitus.

How they achieve contact is a total mystery, but they clearly do. Apparently the cooling effect prolongs the level of satisfaction, and, on emerging, the applause from other members reminds them of their celebrity days. (They don't even have to remove the fridge contents, although Mrs Tibble did discover what she believed to be an impression of Mr Ivanov's buttock on her slab of butter, so residents take care to keep everything in the fridge well wrapped.).

3.Mr Sidney Slott, a retired circus trick-cyclist, (and unfortunately also a unretired sex-maniac), spends most of his Sundays cycling round our Sunshine Home garden on his unicycle offering female members a sexual experience in which they sit balanced on his lap for his 'Ride of the Century'. Mr Slott claims he can bring his passengers to full orgasm within 30 pedals, and, bearing in mind the rather bumpy state of our garden, he may be right.

I can provide several other examples if necessary. May I respectfully ask you to reconsider your directive as far as our premises are concerned, as it is clearly not appropriate for members of this establishment.

Yours faithfully,

Melinda Spilsworthy (Matron)

P.S. I am writing this letter while availing myself of Mr Slott's services, so please excuse the slightly uneven writing.

THE CAIRO HEALTH AND SAFETY EXECUTIVE
HEALTH AND SAFETY HOUSE, 23-27 ABDULLA DRIVE, WEST CAIRO

The Lord Hemiunu
Vizier and Chief Architect
Royal Palace of King Khufu
Avenue of the Sphinxes, Giza

25th April, 2548 B.C.

Greetings, Lord Humiunu

I am writing to you concerning the building of His Majesty's pyramid that has begun recently on the Giza Plateau. I understand this project is your responsibility.

Your novel design makes this the first pyramid with sides sloping at a 52 degree angle from the horizontal. Having received many complaints from the Giza Pyramid Workers Union, we have fully investigated the matter. In our considered view, this represents a serious health and safety issue, particularly when the highly polished 'casing' stones are in place.

As the construction progresses, requiring your workers to clamber about on this slippery limestone surface at such an acute angle is extremely dangerous, particularly when the structure will eventually reach over 100 cubits in height.

Our intention was to demand that you stop work immediately and change the shape of the structure. However, I understand that "he whose majestic light outshines the morning sun" is very keen on your 52 degree design. So, as I have no wish to feel the caress of the strangling rope), I have had my research team diligently investigate other possible solutions.

While seeking ways of creating better grip on the pyramid surface, quite by chance we discovered the friction-creating properties of fresh camel dung and beer. (A 75% / 25% mix is ideal). As a result of this discovery, we require you to arrange for each worker to carry a small bucket of this mixture while on the pyramid surface, into which he must dip his hands and feet at regular intervals. It is important that this is done no less than half-hourly because, as the mixture dries, the friction effect wears off.

Please confirm that you will implement these instructions without delay.

Yours faithfully

Geoffrey Sneferu

Chief Health and Safety Officer

South Lancashire Tiddlywinks Association
'Shangri-La', 3 Station Road, South Bromsgrove, Manchester M34 8RD

Mr Reginald Froggett
Manchester Health and Safety Executive
23-28 York Avenue
Manchester M3 6JS

28th September 1977

Dear Mr Froggett

I am responding to your letter of the 23rd inst. May I firstly protest that your organisation inserted an undercover spy into our Association.

Fortunately your Mr Ponsenby's play exposed him virtually immediately as a fraud. It was observed that his 'squidger' was larger that normal, and on close examination it was discovered to be made of carbon-fibre, (a banned material under national rules). At a subsequent formal club meeting he was required to stand at attention and get out his 'squidger', which was taken from him and ceremonially snapped in two. He was then drummed out of the Association.

I come now to your report and directive based on Mr Ponsenby's observations. It is correct, that a lady member suffered two unfortunate accidents during Mr Ponsenby's visit. Mrs Gladys Thompson was given a black eye by Mr George Jones' wink (while he was trying for a 'boondock'). Later, while exclaiming at Mr Jones' skill, she opened her mouth at the wrong moment and and Mr Jones' wink flew down her throat.

Showing commendabled initiative, Mr Jones, (a part-time St John's Ambulance volunteer), immediately used both arms to encircle Mrs Thompson from behind, lock his hands, and squeeze her chest. (The well-known 'Heimlich' manoeuvre). The resulting violent exhalation of air successfully expelled the wink, but it unfortunately also caused Mrs Thompson's complete upper set to fly across the room, giving another member a nasty gash on the nose. Mrs Thompson was othwise unharmed, and has apparently offered Mr Jones the opportunity to hone his 'Heimlich' skills on her whenever the mood takes him.

This was an isolated incident, and we feel that your ruling requiring all our members to wear swimming goggles and surgical masks while playing, is excessive.

Yours faithfully

Jeremy Buntington

Director S.L.T

Bethsaida & District Health & Safety Directorate
Fifth Floor, Local Government Buildings, Bethsaida, Galilee

Mr Peter (previously Simon)
23 The Lodgings, North Bethsaida
29th September Anno Domini 534

Dear Mr Peter,

We understand that last Thursday, 23rd September, you and some colleagues were in a boat on the Sea of Galilee near Bethsaida when a storm blew up and you got into difficulties.

On the shore at the time was a Mr Jesus. According to information provided by another bystander, Mr J. Iscariot, this Mr Jesus noticed your plight and proceeded to leave the shore and walk towards you on the surface of the water without a boat or any visible means of support.

We would point out that this irresponsible action was taken without any prior Health & Safety permission or notices being issued (which is statutory procedure), and we are therefore seeking to contact Mr Jesus.

Your own behaviour in jumping out of your boat and attempting to emulate Mr Jesus' actions was foolish but perhaps excusable, and clearly demonstrate the ease with which his trick could have encouraged others, both on the shore and in boats, to follow suit, with possible major loss of life.

Our records show that Mr Jesus is not registered with the Bethsaida Council as an illusionist or entertainer, and he therefore has no public liability insurance cover. When you got into difficulties, in the event that he failed to get you back into your boat, (which we are pleased to note that he did), your family would not have been able to claim legal compensation on your behalf.

For Health and Safety reasons, you will appreciate that we need to contact Mr Jesus without delay. So if he is a friend of yours, can you advise us of his current whereabouts? His last recorded address was The Old Stables, The Donkey and Manger Inn, Nazareth, but our letters to him at this address have been returned marked 'Gone away to save The Israelites'.

Apart from the problem of other people risking their lives by emulating Mr Jesus' highly irresponsible trick, the Bethsaida Chamber of Commerce has asked us to point out that his action has led to an immediate drop in local boat hire business, and that an entrepreneur who planned to set up a pedalo hire network throughout this part of the Sea of Galilee has gone bankrupt.

Yours faithfully

Bartholomew the Good

Health & Safety Executive

East Ham Health and Safety Directorate

107 Brick Lane, London E15

Mr J. Thomas
Manpower Erection Services
48A Gardenia Avenue
Plastow, London E12 8GD   3rd April 1973

Dear Mr Thomas

We have received a number of complaints recently from members of the public about your services. Admittedly one was from a person wanting to hire scaffolding, but the others concern serious health and service issues.

These complaints relate to your "Eastern Promise" erection ointment. The complainants say that, not only did it fail to provide the benefit for which they purchased it, but it also caused an unpleasant stinging sensation.

Under Health and Safety legislation, we therefore require you to cease marketing your present ointment formulation. However, we don't wish unreasonably to restrict your business. One who wrote and complained about your product, a Mr Higgins of Dagenham, told us that he subsequently discovered a recipe involving purely natural ingredients that worked for him. As we understand that you refunded Mr Higgins his money, he has stated that he has no objection to our passing his recipe on to you, which is as follows:-

"Mix a quantity of dry domestic starch and yeast in a 3:1 ratio in a small jar. When treatment is required, take a tablespoon of the mixture and add a little water, then smooth the paste onto the member. The self-raising qualities of the yeast, coupled with the stiffening effect of the starch, should create an impressive erection in not more than fifteen minutes. If an accelerated result is required, the member can then be warmed with a hair dryer or on a radiator for 30 seconds".

Please acknowledge this notice and confirm what action you plan to take.

Yours faithfully,

Percival Crabtree (Senior Health and Safety Inspector)

P.S. I tried it, and it jolly well works, but you might get a few crumbs!

London Health and Safety Executive
Forth Floor, Northcliffe House, The Strand, London

Mr Edgar Pinchbeck
Pinchbeck & Tweedle (Importers)
23-27 Weavers Wharf
Wapping, London   1st December Anno Domini 1297

Dear Mr Pinchbeck

We understand your company is importing the newly invented 'spectacles' from Italy, and that you have supplied same to His Majesty, King Edward, and several other key personages of the realm. The King's private secretary has written to us suggesting that your 'spectacles' represent a serious safety risk to his royal personage.

Because of his failing eyesight, His Majesty decided to wear your 'spectacles' for the first time at the battle at Sterling Bridge last week against the Scottish outlaw, William Wallace. On taking his position on the field at the head of the English army, His Majesty called for his 'spectacles' in order to study the Scottish line of battle.

Unfortunately, your 'spectacles' gave the King the impression that the rebels were much closer that His Majesty expected, and he immediately called for his archers to loose a volley at extremely short range. The English Cavalry were charging at the time and this resulted in several English knights receiving painful back and posterior arrow wounds. As if this wasn't enough, William Wallace was heard to shout at the king "With they spectacles, ye're more 'shortshanks' than 'longshanks'". This offensive remark displeased His Highness more than somewhat.

Since the King has subsequently been wearing his spectacles with the side bars hooked over his ears, Her Majesty, Lady Eleanor, apparently suggested that they are actually pulling the King's ears forward, spoiling his looks. (It is perhaps likely that The Queen's remark were due to pique, following the King's overheard observation on seeing Lady Eleanor's face clearly for the first time, which was "My horse's arse is more handsome".

In a second situation, last week at Tyburn our chief executioner, Rufus Pierpoint, wore his new 'spectacles' for the first time to carry out the beheading of another Scottish terrorist. Unfortunately, he not only missed the terrorist's neck with his axe, but also partially severed his own big toe. What's more, in the ensuing furore, the prisoner escaped.

Yours faithfully

Hugo de Vere Thomas

Health & Safety Director

Post Script: Incidentally, should you be seeking a 'Royal Appointment' warrant from His Majesty for your 'spectacles', unless you'd like to be the next candidate for Mr Pierpoint, I'd drop the idea!

Durham Health and Safety Executive
89-94 The Parade, Coalpit Road, Durham

Mr John Walker
Apothecary
59 High Street, Stockton-on-Tees   17th May 1827

Dear Mr Walker

May we firstly offer congratulations on your invention of your "strike anywhere matches". We understand these are small wooden sticks coated with antimony sulfide, potassium chlorate and other chemicals, and can be rubbed against any rough surface whereupon they burst into flame. They are therefore a boon to pipe, cigar and cigarette smokers. However we write to you today for health and safety reasons.

The first case concerns Mr Justice Mountebank Q.C., who was sitting at Durham Assizes two weeks ago. According to His Lordship, having completed a long day in court, he retired to his chambers and to help him relax, he clipped the end of a Havana Corona and put it in his mouth. Finding no convenient abrasive surface to hand, and being of a hirsute disposition, he decided to test your "strike anywhere" claim by rubbing your match down his own cheek.

As your promotional leaflet claims, it immediately flared into flame, but unfortunately it also set light to his wig, and his manservant had to speedily empty a bucket of water over His Lordship to save him from harm. While His Lordship was none the worse for his ordeal, one cannot say the same about his wig!

The second case concerns Mildred Flook, a prostitute from 17a The Buildings, Gasworks View, Stockton, who was 'promenading' along Harbour Road last Friday night. Having purchased a box of your matches, she paused to light her cigarette, striking one against the top of her whalebone corset. As the match flared, it unfortunately set light to the tissue paper padding in her brassier. It was lucky for Miss Flook that a passing sailor rushed to her aid and, with his bare hands, bravely patted the whole of her upper body to beat out the flames, (somewhat over-enthusiastically, according to Miss Flook).

The third case concerns horse breeder, Mr Alfred Snaffle, of 'The Ranch', Slag Heap Rise, Durham. While out exercising one of his mares, he decided to light a cigar by striking one of your matches across his buttock. Unbeknown to him, this caused a tiny piece of glowing match-head to drop into his rear pocket.

It was only later when Mr Snaffle's groin began to sweat and chafe that he realised something was amiss. (This worried him somewhat as three weeks earlier he had entertained Miss Flook). However, on returning to the stables, he was relieved to find that sitting in the horse trough for ten minutes extinguished the problem.

Together with other similar cases about which we have been notified, these demonstrate that your "strike anywhere matches" can be a serious health and safety risk. To avoid prosecution, please advise what action you intend to take.

Yours faithfully,

Nigel Brass-Farthing

Health and Safety Executive

Empire Health and Safety Directorate

The Foreign Office, Parliament Square, London

Mr L. J. Silver
c/o The Spyglass Inn
23 Tides Reach, Wapping

1st September, 1754

Dear Mr Silver,

We understand that you own a tame African parrot called "Captain Flint". We have received information from a Mr James Hawkins, of 72 Cosham Road, Portsmouth, that during your last voyage to Hispaniola you made a practice of encouraging "Captain Flint" to perch on your shoulder, (and the shoulders of Mr Hawkins and other members of your crew).

Recent medical research have shown this to be an extremely dangerous practice, in that African parrots carry 'High Pathogenic Avian Influenza' virus (HPAIV), and that a bite from their beaks can convey this dangerous virus to human beings. We cannot overstress this matter. HPAIV can cause both blindness and permanent loss of sensation or even atrophy of one or more limbs. Mr Hawkins tells us you have a glass eye and wooden leg, so I suspect our warning may have come too late!

We are responsible for protecting you, Mr Hawkins, and any other English members of your crew from this problem during your next voyage.

Clearly, one cannot stop parrots from pecking, but allowing them to perch in close proximity to ears necks and other human flesh is therefore to be actively discouraged. They must be prevented from perching on peoples' shoulders at all costs. On all voyages your stores will include beef dripping. So we feel the best solution is that you and your men liberally smear dripping on your shoulders each morning, which will prevent your, (or any), parrot from getting a foothold.

Unfortunately, after a few days in the sun, the beef dripping takes on an aroma best described as exotic. However, in view of the poor personal hygiene among English sailors, we consider these drawbacks represent a small price to pay to protect their health.

Please confirm that you will adopt this ruling prior to your next voyage.

Yours faithfully,

Horatio Fortescue-Brown

Health and Safety Directorate - Overseas Territories

West of England Health and Safety Directorate

County Council Offices, 23 –54 The High Street, Tiverton, Devon

Mr Percy Green, Chief Executive
The English Morris Dancers Association
23 Piccadilly, London   2nd June, Anno Domini 1459

Dear Mr Green

We need to draw your attention to hitherto unrecognised health and safety issues regarding your members' dancing activities. We have covertly inspected several performances, and some activities contravene regulations.

Firstly, we refer to the case of Mr L. Humphries of the Cornish Morris Dancers branch. On the 4th April this year, during the dance's traditional foot stamping movements, the string holding the bells around Mr Humphries' right leg broke and the bells fell to the ground. Some of these rolled under the feet of other dancers, caused two slipped discs and a hernia. We have concluded that the only way to avoid this dangerous situation is to ban the wearing of the bells. Instead, when the dancers stamp the ground, (when the bells would normally ring), we suggest the dancers sing out "Ding" or "Ting" in unison, in keeping with the spirit of the dance.

Secondly is the behaviour of your Morris dancing "Fool" and his pig's bladder. While he is of course a traditional Morris character, and the bladder is usually applied to dancers' bottoms, we must point out that this constitutes a major safety risk if used on other parts of the body. This was demonstrated at the Morris dance in Sidmouth, South Devon, last Friday, when an over-inflated bladder caught Mr George Smith in the face, causing him a severe nosebleed requiring treatment by the local witch. At the time of writing, his false teeth have also not been found.

We don't wish to ban the bladder, but it is clear that the inflation pressure needs to be regulated. Our subsequent tests showed that 87 p.s.i. is the highest acceptable pressure. So, prior to any Morris dance, the team member playing the 'Fool' will need to take his bladder to his nearest blacksmith and have it adjusted to the above pressure. For public liability protection he must also obtain a pressure certificate signed by the blacksmith.

Yours faithfully

Henry Bolsworthy
Health & Safety Director

Essex Health and Safety Directorate

Council Offices, High Street, Chelmsford, Essex CM3 3PU

Mr S. Claus
23 Aurora Avenue
Rovaniemi
Lapland

1st January 1843

Dear Mr Claus

While we recognise that you carry out an important annual function, it has come to our notice that, while making your deliveries, suspending your reindeer team and sleigh at a height, we understand, of about 50 feet above residential areas of Essex can result in endangering the safety of the public.

You will, I'm sure, appreciate that while travelling across the sky, reindeer do not normally evacuate their bowels, but wait for a convenient stopping place, (as we ourselves do). This means that coming to a halt and remaining suspended above the ground for a few minutes represents an ideal defecation opportunity for them.

However, it has only now been recognised that this can be extremely dangerous for anyone on the ground below. This has been revealed by our testing team who borrowed a fully-grown reindeer for Colchester Zoo, and used a crane to lift it to 50 feet to measure excrement velocity. Unfortunately they then waited three hours before defecation took place, during which time the creature urinated several times over our team, causing a stinging sensation to the skin and blotches that have taken days to subside.

When the defecation moment finally arrived, to be honest, our team were unprepared for the volume and weight of the deposit. One person suffered concussion. For your information the impact velocity was calculated at over 70 miles per hour.

Mr Claus - while we appreciate that it's only for one night per year, your activities are a serious infringement of Health and Safety laws.

Seeking an answer, our tests have shown that it has been impossible to train our representative reindeer to clench its buttocks when stationary, in spite of quite dangerous trials, during which one of our more adventurous team members lost a gold signet ring and his mother's rubber glove.

Our conclusion is that there is only one workable solution. If you wish to continue to make your annual deliveries to Essex, you need to ensure that during your journey from Lapland your reindeer empty their bowels while in flight over the North Sea or unpopulated land areas. Our further tests on our reindeer have shown that he could be stimulated to do this by prodding his rear end gently with a piece of holly attached to the end of your whip. So that seems to be the solution there.

We now come to the equally serious matter of your own toiletry habits, (and sense of humour).

Simply leaving your sleigh and sitting on a convenient chimney pot is certainly not acceptable. Mrs Johnston, of 27 Chrysanthemum Avenue, Chingford, who wrote to us, was less than amused by your actions, and the Christmas card you left, saying "Here's a little extra present you weren't expecting", was hardly in keeping with the yuletide spirit. We'll be forwarding her bills for a new carpet and a shampoo for her poodle, 'Mitzi'.

Please respond before December next with your proposals for dealing with this matter.

Yours faithfully,

Rodney Pottington

Health and safety Executive

Olney Pancake Race Association

Hon. Sec: Mrs R. Duckworth, 'Mon Repos', 5 The Avenue, Olney, Buckinghamshire

Mr Hubert Pring
Buckinghamshire Health and Safety Executive
28-30 The Parade, Aylesbury   20th February, 1465

Dear Mr Pring

We were very concerned to receive your letter of the 15th February. The Olney Pancake Race has been a Shrove Tuesday tradition in our village since 1445, when local resident, Agatha Witherinton, was finishing up her accumulated cooking fat before the start of Lent, and lost track of time. She heard the church bell start to peal for the 'Shriving' service, and had to run to the church with her pan, tossing the pancake on the way to prevent it burning.

And the tradition has lasted. We had 32 participants at last Wednesday's race, to which you refer. Let me respond to the event as follows.

It is true that while participating in the race, Mrs Toddlemarsh of Drover's Cottage, sustained a blow to the head. The competitor immediately in front of her, Mrs Threadneedle, had used insufficient fat to cook her pancake and it stuck to her pan. Trying to toss it with greasy hands, she lost her grip on the pan and the whole thing flew into the air. Unfortunately, it descended on Mrs Toddlemarsh, striking her a glancing blow to the forehead.

It could not have been a heavy or disabling blow as you insinuate, because, after a slight stumble, Mrs Toddlemarsh continued running. What was unfortunate, I will admit, is that the impact dislodged the pancake from the pan which wrapped itself round her face, resulting in a severe coughing fit.

As this was a happening of pure chance, your ruling that pans should be banned, and that pancakes should not be tossed but simply carried under the arms of contestants is frankly ridiculous. In addition, pancakes that have been carried a hundred yards under the armpits of perspiring participants will produce a flavour I suspect will be too sophisticated for the palates of our menfolk!

Yours faithfully

Rosamund Duckworth

Secretary – O.P.R.A.

The London Hippodrome

Leicester Square, London, WC2   Reservations: 02703 393482

Mr Percival Bolt
Central London Health and Safety Executive
23-25 Charing Cross Road, London WC1   29th January 1900

 Dear Mr Bolt

Thank you for your recent letter referring to the Grand Gala Opening of our new circus on the 15th inst, which included performing elephants for the first time in England. As you can imagine, we were delighted that the evening attracted a large audience, including being honoured by the presence of the Lord Mayor of London and his family who sat in the front row.

In reply to your letter, we indeed recognise the gravity of the unfortunate incident that occurred during the show when 'Rajah', our 5 ton Indian bull elephant, while skilfully balancing on his front legs in the ring, and trumpeting in tune with the national anthem, with no warning discharged a heavy jet of excrement over the first two rows of the audience. (While elephants are vegetarians, I appreciate that this did not lessen the distress and panic caused, and represents a serious health and safety issue.

I have now fully investigated the matter. Apparently three days prior to the opening, Rajah's trainer, Mr Henry Gupta, had noticed he was sluggish and diagnosed constipation. Mr Gupta immediately dosed Rajah by mouth with a mixture of sennapods and syrup of figs. Rajah soon appeared to be back to his old self. However, in the absence of any 'concrete' results, the night prior to the grand opening, in desperation Mr Gupta gave Rajah anally four enemas and a gallon of warm virgin olive oil. Here again there appeared to be no effect.

While undoubtedly the act was expected to be our star attraction, in hindsight, it's unfortunate that Mr Gupta decided that Rajah should be included in the gala opening. The effect was also exacerbated because, at the critical moment, Rajah was balancing on his front feet. So the height and position of Rajah's anus was over 15 feet from the ground, and almost vertical, and this resulted in a significant coverage of the audience.

Poor old Rajah! In retrospect, it also now becomes clear that his enthusiastic trumpeting of the National Anthem was as much an expression of relief as a musical accompaniment!

To prevent the situation reoccurring I am pleased to tell you that Mr Gupta has come up with the answer. He has purchased from a motor parts supplier a tyre pressure gauge with which, (with the help of a stepladder and in my view considerable courage), he can determine the anal pressure of each elephant, prior to including it in the performance, and will exclude any animal showing a dangerous excess. I trust this solution will be acceptable.

Yours sincerely,

Wilberfore Bonaparte

Proprietor - London Hippodrome Circus

Humberside Health and Safety Executive

Plantagenet House, South Parade, Hartlepool, West Yorkshire

Mr Julian Fortescue
Chief Conductor – The Grimsby Symphony Orchestra
The Leisure Centre
Grimsby, West Yorkshire   12th February 1975

Dear Mr Fortescue

We have received a complaint from a Mrs Agnes Phibes on behalf of her husband, Mr Percival Phibes, who we understand is your orchestra's senior cellist. This involved an unfortunate occurrence while he was performing his cello solo during the new 'Midnight in Hades' symphony at Grimsby Town Hall on the 5th February.

Mrs Phibes has advised us that after her husband's final rehearsal for this new work, the Hungarian composer, (who'd come to England especially to attend the performance), decided that he wanted the last movement of the solo to be played an octave lower that he had originally scored. While this involved playing a 'Bottom C', an exceptionally low note for the cello, (which had not been rehearsed), Mr Phibes had not considered it a problem. As you appreciate, unlike other stringed instruments the cello is played clasped between the musician's knees, and the vibrations created in the body of the instrument are therefore in close proximity to the groin. Apparently, during the performance, Mr Phibes played this amended, last movement without a hitch and all seemed to go well.

What is now clear is that the playing of this 'Bottom C' note had unfortunately set up an inaudible vibration in his genitalia. This continued for some time after its source stopped – in fact long after the end of the performance. Mr Phibes was even conscious of the vibration on the bus ride home, although he states that he was not concerned as it was actually a somewhat pleasant sensation.

However, a more serious aspect is that while Mrs Phibes was doing their laundry she noticed that the underpants her husband had been wearing during the performance had been scorched. From our subsequent tests it is now clear that this was a result of the heat build-up created by Mr Phibes' genitalia vibration. Clearly, this represents a serious health and safety issue.

Page 66

Our research team have looked into possible solutions. One idea that initially appeared promising involved the artist suspending a bag of ice cubes on a string inside his trousers for the performance of the piece. While in tests this prevented the heat build-up, the condensation also leaked down the performer's legs, upsetting his vibrato.

Another important finding of our tests was that not all of our sample cello players experienced this genitalia vibration when the relevant note was played.

So our technical team have come up with a simple tuning fork that reproduces this 'Bottom C' note. (I enclose a sample fork). Local orchestras planning to play 'Midnight in Hades' can buy one of these for £4.50 from our Humberside offices. Their male cellist can strike it against any hard surface and then place against his groin to check possible effects prior to the performance. (As Mr Phibes noted, far from being painful, the vibration is an unusually pleasant sensation). In the event that he is susceptible to this vibration, to stay within Health and Safety rules the cellist will have to play the solo 'side-saddle'.

Yours faithfully,

Stephen Middleditch

Senior Health and Safety Officer

P.S. Since these tuning forks were mentioned in the Grimsby Evening Clarion this week, we have sold over a thousand. We had no idea that there were so many cellists in Grimsby.

English Health and Safety Directorate

Health and Safety House, 23-27 Shaftesbury Avenue, London WC1

Mr Henry Fishbaum
Chairman- American Clothing Manufacturers' Association
2400 Times Square
New York, United States of America   12th November 1914

Dear Mr Fishbaum

      Our role is to protect the health and safety of English people. We are therefore writing to express concern about Mr Sundbach's recent invention of the "hook-less fastener" (or 'Zip' as it is becoming known), and the fact that many of your member companies have started fitting them instead of buttons in their trouser production. Our reasons are as follows:-

1. The speed with which the 'Zip' enables the wearer to undo his or her lower garment is excessive from a moral viewpoint. As our Archbishop of Canterbury points out, your 'Zip' significantly increases the opportunity for lower classes to engage in illicit sexual activity, (or 'coitus opportunisticus ' as he describes it), potentially leading to an explosion in promiscuity. The charity, "Save English Virgins from Sin", has also expressed serious concern.

2. Our Police Commissioner is also worried that the speed of the 'Zip' action will lead to a big increase in the unpleasant practice of 'flashing' that has developed on Hampstead Heath and other parts of London.

3. While we appreciate the urination facility argument, the positioning of your 'Zips' on men's' trousers is also of serious concern on pure safety grounds, in that they are being fitted at the front, in close proximity to the male reproductive organ. Having obtained a pair of trousers with a 'Zip', our tests have shown that unless the opening or closing operation is carried out slowly, and with good muscular control, an extremely painful 'knitting' of the skin and the 'Zip' can occur. (Mr Parsons, our researcher spent two days in hospital being 'unravelled').

      In view of the above, should any of your members apply to our Board of Trade to import these trousers, we will vigorously oppose such applications.

Yours faithful

Henry Snodland

Senior Health and Safety Office

Winchester Health and Safety Executive

Area Headquarters, The Parade, Camelot, Winchester

His Majesty Arthur
High King of the Britons
The Palace
Camelot   6th April, Anno Domini 529

Majesty, greetings,

Knights' Tilting Contest – Injury Case No 423 / Sir Galahad

May we respectfully draw your attention to the case of Sir Galahad, who has written to us following his unseating during the joust at Camelot on 24th March.

While the Executive recognises that these events enable your knights to practice their battle skills, in spite of Sir Galahad's armour, his opponent's lance caused him heavy chest bruising and led to consequent heart palpitations.

As this is one of several similar cases, it is clear that using rigid wooden lances for tilting practice constitutes a serious health and safety risk to your knights.

We have therefore decided that from the 1st September this year, all such lances are banned from tilting contests. By that date they must be replaced with heavy-duty rubber lances of not less than 2029 p.s.i. tensile strength. This is based on our tests which have clearly shown that lances made to this particular specification will register a 'hit', but will bend on impact, preventing serious body damage.

As your Majesty will have appreciated, this ruling actually opens up new entertainment dimensions for your future jousts. For example, in a tilt, at the beginning of his charge, the knight can begin waving his lance from side to side, setting up an oscillation that, on reaching his opponent, can deal a hefty sideways blow, potentially 'swatting' him from the saddle.

As an alternative, immediately before reaching his opponent, a knight may lower and deliberately drive his rubber lance into the ground. Somewhat like a pole-vaulter, his lance will bow, lifting the knight fully out of his saddle. This will not only enable him to dodge his opponent's lance, but, (with practice), to then fall upon the opponent feet first, dealing him a significant blow.

Would Your Majesty kindly pass on these instructions to your knights .

Yours faithfully

Alan Bolingbroke
Health & Safety Director

North English Health & Safety Directorate

Council Chambers, High Street, Sterling, North England

Mr William Wallace
Scots Encampment
Nr Sterling Bridge
North England   15th September Anno Domini 1297

Dear Mr Wallace,

Our directorate is sometimes criticised for failing to recognise talent and innovation, even among our nation's enemies. So may we firstly congratulate you on your strategy at the recent battle of Sterling Bridge. This relates particularly to concealing sharpened wooden stakes in the grass in front of your troops and then suddenly raising them at the moment the charge of the English heavy horse cavalry reached them, successfully impaling many of the riders. We are pleased to advise you that this activity does not contravene our Health and Safety regulations.

However, we are writing to you on another matter. Unlike our troops, you Scots restrict your below-the-waist apparel to 'kilts' with no under-clouts of any kind. We understand that at the commencement of the battle, as the English approached, at a pre-arranged signal all 750 of your front rank suddenly did an about turn and bent over, exposing their unwashed, hairy buttocks to the enemy. This caused considerable shock and distress in the English ranks, and several troops subsequently needed counselling.

While this exposure is in contravention of Health & Safety regulations, in itself, it might have been dealt with by us simply with a formal warning. However, a more serious infringement occurred at this time.

While exposing their buttocks to the English forces, many of your troops unfairly sought to enhance the effect of their action by also passing wind. This foul gas, aided by a stiff, south-easterly wind, drifted over the English lines at several points causing nausea and fainting. The distinctive sound of this release of gas should have alerted the English front ranks, but your forces cunningly masked it by playing their bagpipes. This is a serious contravention of Health & Safety regulations, Section18, para 3, "Noxious gas emissions without prior warning."

Mr Wallace, I am writing to warn you that if you are planning to adopt similar tactics at your next battle, Health and Safety regulations will require you to adopt both the following procedures:-

a) Your front-line troops facing the English must display a warning banner not less than 30 seconds prior to their actions, This must feature the following wording:- "Beware – Imminent buttocks exposure and risk of noxious gases. Listen for the bagpipes".

b) Immediately prior to the action, to provide a screen, each of your troops must remove his bonnet and suspend it in front of his buttocks for the period of the exposure. As some of your troops are of extremely large stature, these particular persons may have to carry a second bonnet to ensure adequate screening. In the event that your troops also pass wind, the bonnets will help to trap the noxious gases.

Yours faithfully,

William Bolingbroke-Smith

Sterling Health & Safety Directorate

P.S. While this does not form part of our responsibilities, as you probably saw, the English wives and camp followers were on the hill behind their army watching the Sterling Bridge battle. Following the exposure, we have received request from several of them to meet, (counting from their left), Scots troops numbers 7, 45, 82, 105 and especially 149 (15 requests), if this can be arranged.

Nottinghamshire Health and Safety Executive

The High Sheriff's Offices, Nottingham,

F. Tuck, Esquire
c/o The 'Merrie Men' Organisation
Sherwood Forest   23rd May 1261

Dear Mr Tuck

According to our records, apart from your religious duties you are health and safety officer for the 'Merrie Men' organisation run by Mr R. Hood. We are therefore writing to you on a serious health and safety matter.

It has come to our notice that when using their longbows, your 'Merrie Men' consistently use their index and second fingers for drawing their bow strings. Bearing in mind the power of these bows, this action puts unreasonable stress on those two digits, and this can lead to joint inflammation and arthritis. In the most serious cases these particular digits can become unusable for any other purpose, and result in a condition known to the archery fraternity as 'Fletcher's fingers'.

As you appreciate, this situation can leave your chief executive, Mr Hood, open to health and safety prosecution. To keep within regulations, we feel it is simply a matter of 'spreading the load', i.e. for your men to use a single finger to draw their bow strings, and to change the finger used daily. So, if a man uses his index finger on a Monday, he needs to use his second finger on a Tuesday, his third finger on a Wednesday and his little finger on a Thursday.

As it is clearly not practical to use thumbs for this purpose, we suggest that your men should avoid fighting on a Friday or at the weekend. For these days perhaps you could encourage other digital activities. Perhaps they could use their bowstrings to play 'Cat's cradle', or join our Friday Yo-Yo circle.

As part of demonstrating your 'Merrie' Men's compliance with the above requirements, it would be helpful if they could be asked to make a 'V' sign with their fingers whenever they encounter my troops.

Yours faithfully

William de Grey

High Sheriff and Health & Safety Director

London Health and Safety Executive

Health and safety House, 12-18 Tides Reach, The Embankment, London

Sir Walter Raleigh
Durham House
The Strand, London   12th July, Anno Domini 1585

Dear Walter

    May I firstly offer my personal congratulations and that of my whole Executive on your knighthood last month. It is indeed an example to us all. Your courtesy and manners could not have been better illustrated than when you met Her Majesty last week at Greenwich. What a gentlemanly gesture to cast your new cloak over that puddle to protect Her Majesty's shoes.

    As your action was of course widely reported, hundreds of other London gentlemen have started to emulate your courteous gesture.

    While in itself this not a a health and safety problem, an element of practical joking has manifested itself amongst the more waggish fraternity. This has taken the form of casting cloaks over quite deep pockets of water, allowing the poor ladies to fall sometimes up to their waists in muddy water. There was one reported instance where a lady in Putney disappeared altogether, and it was only after several persons heaved on the edges of the cloak that she reappeared.

    Sir Walter, if you wish to continue this practice, before casting your cloak we require you first to drop some suitable depth gauge, such as your manservant, into the puddle to check its depth. If it is significant, you may have lost a manservant, but you will not have contravened health and safety regulations.

    Please acknowledge this directive.

Yours sincerely,

Fitz-Hubert

Sir Henry Fitz-Hubert, Chairman

Greater London Health and Safety Executive

Health and Safety Offices, 214-217 Commercial Road, City of London

The Lord Sandwich of Bath, KFG, CBM, DFC.
Grosvenor House,
The Strand, London   21st September 1887

My Lord,

I am responding to your letter dated 28th June regarding the Cuban cigars you purchased recently to celebrate Her Majesty Queen Victoria's Jubilee this year. We understand you feel they represent a health and safety risk.

As you pointed out, these particular cigars are promoted by their makers on the basis that, (quoting from their literature), *"the leaves are rolled on the thighs of virgins glistening with perspiration"*, as the reason why they are of purest quality and easy to draw.

As your Lordship remarked in your letter, good cigars are like fine wine – by holding one under the nose a cigar connoisseur should be able to tell the age of the virgin who rolled it and whether this was carried out on her upper or lower thigh. Clearly this has not been the case here. You state that the cigars you purchased contained what appeared to be human hairs and talcum powder which, when smoked, caused violent coughing and resulted in a badly inflamed throat.

We have now taken up your complaint with the Cuban makers in Havana, who have thoroughly investigated the matter. They have individually checked each person working in their rolling department and have reassured us that each is a virgin.

However, what has come to light is that these leaf rollers are highly skilled employees and they are therefore kept on as long as possible. In fact eight of these virgins are 60 year old women, and one is a man! (Manuel Borrito, a somewhat hirsute individual, apparently holds a doctor's letter confirming that he has never had sexual intercourse).

While the Cuban cigar makers have technically substantiated their "thighs of virgins" claim, it is hardly in the spirit of clarity. We therefore agree that this situation represents a potential health and safety danger, and have pursued the matter with them.

Following our intervention, the cigar makers have transferred Signor Borrito to another department, and have undertaken to ensure that the leaves of all cigars to be exported to England under this brand will be rolled solely by female virgins in their teens.

Incidentally, the makers have also decided that our health and safety intervention has exposed a new marketing opportunity. So, rather than sacking the 60 year old virgins, the cigars they roll will be marketed to the smoker seeking a more mature, vintage experience. Each humidor will carry the message "Unless you've tried what a sixty year old virgin's thighs can offer, you haven't lived".

Yours faithfully

Dudley Wallpole

Health and Safety Executive

North Devon Health and Safety Executive
Executive Headquarters, 13-18 The Avenue, Appledore, North Devon

Mr T. Cobleigh
13A Church Lane
Spreyton, Dartmoor   14th July Anno Domini 1843

Dear Mr Cobleigh,

We have been contacted by Mr Thomas Pearce, a respected citizen, of Hill View, Sticklepath, regarding a serious health and safety matter.

Mr Pearce has informed us that on the 28th June he loaned his 18 hands grey mare to you (and Messrs Brewer, Stewer, Gurney, Davey, Whiddon, and Hawke, (and a person whose name we believe is 'Dawl'.) We understand that you borrowed the mare to enable you all to get to the fair at Widdecombe, a journey of over 12 miles, and to return.

From our understanding of both your outward and return journeys, you and your colleagues infringed health and safety regulations in that none of your party was properly equipped with protective riding hats, stirrups, or saddle, and that at least one person was actually sitting back to front during the journey.

According to several Widdecombe hostelries, at the commencement of your return journey some of your guests appeared unstable. In the opinion of the various landlords, this was due to the absence of a saddle, and in no way connected with your party's substantial consumption of Widdecombe scrumpi, which they understood to be part of a countywide sampling survey.

Please provide your early response to our above statements. On another matter, we are required to pass copies of our case notes to the Devon Highways Authority who will be contacting you, as the mounting of eight men on one horse falls foul of their 'Vehicle Overloading' regulations.

Yours faithfully

Samuel Carter

Senior Investigator

Romania Health & Safety Directorate

Council Offices, 3-7 Frankenstein Avenue, North Wallachia

Majesty Of All He Surveys, Prince Vladimir
King (and Prime Minister) of Wallachia
The Royal Palace
Wallachia, Romania   1st December in the year 1461

Greetings, Majesty,

While we don't wish to be disrespectful, we must once again draw your Majesty's attention to the fact that your favourite punishment of impalement for your errant citizens contravenes Romania's health and safety regulations.

Keen to avoid such treatment ourselves, we would have hesitated to raise the matter with your Majesty at this time. However, in your role of Prime Minister you are of course facing a general election this January, and we understand from the latest readership survey that your popularity rating is apparently at an all-time low. (This may conceivably be a reflection of your impalement activities).

Your Majesty, we also bring good tidings. We have come up with a solution, i.e. a punishment that will create the same level of terror as impalement, while at the same time avoid contravening health and safety regulations.

Having tested a number of options on the prisoners you kindly loaned us for the purpose, two ideas have worked best. These are a) colonic irrigate using a well-shaken bottle of champagne ; or, b) the application of an extra large enema wrapped in holly. Our recommendation is the extra large enema with holly. While it is clearly a cheaper option than champagne, it is also recognised by the Romanian Medical Association as a treatment for extreme constipation.

The 'holly' component might also appeal to your Majesty because, apart from its extraordinary scouring qualities, it offers an appropriate seasonal theme for your re-election campaign.

We look forward to hearing that you are willing to make this change.

Yours faithfully

Stanislaus Dobrovski

Health & Safety Executive

Westminster Health and Safety Directorate
24-28 Fleet Street, London W2 4DR

William Thomas Esq.
Proprietor - Bridge View Guest House
No 12, London Bridge North Side,
Westminster, London W2 3HR   17th August 1858

Dear Sir or Madam,

EMERGENCY 'PASS IT ON' SCHEME

It is necessary to write to you as a local London Bridge resident and guest-house operator on what is unfortunately an urgent and distasteful matter.

The increasing popularity of the new 'flush' lavatories in London has lead to a build-up of concentrated human waste entering the Thames, (as opposed to previously when chamber pots were emptied out of windows). This has resulted in a significant excrement build-up that the high tides have not been able to disperse.

As if this wasn't enough, exacerbated by the very warm weather at present, there is also a very unpleasant stench in this area, (as you will be aware!). The Times has dubbed this 'The Great Stink'.

However, from a health and safety viewpoint, the stench is not the most serious problem.

At the ten-seater public lavatory at Rotherhythe, (that normally drains perfectly well into the Thames), a man who had dropped his glass eye into the pan and was searching for it with a lighted candle, ignited a pocket of sewer gas accumulated in the pipe beneath the lavatories. This caused a violent blow-back which temporarily elevated three other incumbents from their seats. All three have subsequently complained of a lack of sensation in the exposed parts, and are seeking compensation from Westminster City Council.

Clearly, immediate and unprecedented measures are required to reducing the amount of excrement being deposited into the Thames until the backlog clears.

We therefore require you to take the following action immediately :-

All your guests, staff and family must adopt what we have called our "PASS IT ON" scheme. This involves ceasing to flush all lavatories at your premises forthwith. Instead you and they must start using expandable waterproof envelopes, (sample enclosed), obtainable from our offices free of charge, including first class postage.

As part of each individual evacuation these must be filled with the waste, sealed, and then posted to any of the depositor's family, friends or acquaintances who live at least 10 miles outside London.

Envelopes must be marked with the sender's name and address for recognition purposes.

You are required to instigate this procedure with immediate effect. Please acknowledge this letter.

Yours faithfully

Hugo Makepeace

Westminster Health & Safety Directorate

Encl: 1st class postage envelope sample.

London Hernia Sufferers Association
First Floor, 24 The Parade, Stepney Green, London *(Members please use stair lift)*

Sir Rupert Cromwell Bart.
The London Health and Safety Executive
248-250 City Road,
London   15th February Anno Domini 521

Dear Sir Rupert,

Like everyone in the Kingdom, we at the L.H.S.A. shared the national interest in which of our worthy Gentlemen at Arms would succeed to the throne when King Uther Pendragon passes on.

It was an excellent idea, (thought up by the court magician, Merlin, we understand), to set up that huge stone anvil with the golden sword embedded in it, with the promise that the Gentleman who was able to remove it would be the successor to the throne.

As you know, this matter was meant to be settled on Christmas Day last year, but, unfortunately only one of the many Gentlemen who participated was successful - young Arthur, the King's son. However, as he was not titled, he was not deemed to be an acceptable candidate, and the contest was repeated at Candlemas, on the second of this month. Here too, only Arthur was successful, and (having proved it twice), he was then proclaimed successor.

However, there has been an unfortunate spin-off from the above.

Many of the Gentlemen attempting the task adopted the position of placing their feet either side of the sword, bending forward to grasp the hilt, and then heaving backwards. Unfortunately, this is one of the classic ways of getting a hernia.

I am writing on behalf of a number of important Gentlemen at Arms who have experienced significant problems following their attempts.

I cite three representative cases as follows:-

•Sir Ector can no longer mount his war horse without the assistance of six pages and a small crane.

•Sir Lancelot now finds it very difficult to sit at the Round Table at Camelot for the weekly meetings, and Lady Guinevere has had to knit him a large swan's down cushion.

•Sir Kay can no longer lift his battle lance above knee-height, (and Lady Kay has told us in confidence that that's not the only lance with which he is having trouble!)

While I am personally delighted that our membership subscriptions and sales of our house magazine, "Truss Troubles", have risen substantially following the contest, we respectfully suggest that you should be investigating this situation as a serious health and safety matter.

Yours faithfully

Henry Belvedere

Chief Executive

East Surbiton Flamenco Club
c/o Mr Manuel Bogotá, 7 Station Road, Surbiton.
Fellow of the Barcelona Flamenco Academy,

Señor G. Dumbleton
Greater London Health and Safety Executive
15-24 High Street, Kingston-upon-Thames   20th November 1977

Honoured Señor Dumbleton

Please excuse that my English is not good. We receive your letter of 14th November, which has caused nausea among our members.

It is correct that when your inspectors raid our club on Saturday night 12th November, Mr George Thomson was on stage entertaining large audience with his renowned two-minute castanet solo. Your inspectors say Mr Thomson's playing "caused palm inflammation and blisters on his index and middle fingers".

However, Mr Thomson wish me point out that these injuries were in fact a result of his competing in the Surbiton Beer Drinking Contest at the 'Jolly Sailor', Micham, the previous evening, when he drink 18 pints of your English beer very quick. Mr Thomson explain this to your inspectors at the time, but they no accept.

In your letter you demand that all our club's Flamenco dancers replace one of their traditional hardwood castanets with a rubber one, "**to prevent damaging vibration and chafing**". With respect, your ruling would result in removal of the 'click' sound, which would mean a totally silencio performance, and that would destroy Flamenco's traditional impact.

So, I now suggest compromise what we believe meet your requirements.

Our members are prepared to wear surgical rubber gloves while playing their castanets, so the famous 'click' will not be lost. Some of our aficionados feel they will actually enhance our Flamenco. For example, last week Mrs Florence Smith wore a pair when practising in her sitting room, and both she and her husband say that they improved her performance. (Unfortunately Mr Smith has latent rubber fetish, so he should not be taken too seriously).

Señor, we look forward to your agreements to our proposal.

Yours, with multo pleasure, Señor,

Manuel Bogota

M. Bogotá - Technical Director

International Media Acclaim

"Genuinely brought tears to my eyes."
Inverness Times (Health Correspondent)

"A landmark approach to a sensitive subject."
'Truss Troubles Monthly'

"Writing to warm the cockles!"
Ferret Owners Journal

"A breakthrough in international productivity."
Turkish Castration Chronicle

"Absolutely magic writing"
Welsh Druids Weekly

"A stiff challenge to other humour writers"
The World of Yeast Annual

"Gives a whole new meaning to virgin's thighs"
Cigar Smokers' Monthly

www.ingramcontent.com/pod-product-compliance
Lightning Source LLC
Chambersburg PA
CBHW071355090426
42738CB00012B/3126